W9-AVI-357

About the Author

Caroline Dow has been a tea leaf reader and herbalist for thirty years, and conducts popular workshops on tea leaf reading all over the country. She is the author of fourteen books and is the owner and manager of a successful herbal mail order company. Visit her blog online at www.carolinedowbooks .com/teablog.

To Write to the Author

If you wish to contact the author or would like more information about this book, please write to the author in care of Llewellyn Worldwide, and we will forward your request. Both the author and the publisher appreciate hearing from you and learning of your enjoyment of this book and how it has helped you. Llewellyn Worldwide cannot guarantee that every letter written to the author can be answered, but all will be forwarded. Please write to:

Caroline Dow
℅ Llewellyn Worldwide
2143 Wooddale Drive
Woodbury, MN 55125-2989, U.S.A.
Please enclose a self-addressed stamped envelope for reply,
or $1.00 to cover costs. If outside the U.S.A., enclose
an international postal reply coupon.

Many of Llewellyn's authors have websites with additional information and resources. For more information, please visit our website at:
www.llewellyn.com

Tea Leaf
Reading
For Beginners

Tea Leaf Reading

For Beginners

Your Fortune in a Teacup

CAROLINE DOW

Llewellyn Publications
Woodbury, Minnesota

First Edition
First Printing, 2011

Cover design by Adrienne Zimiga
Cover photo © 2009 by iStockphoto.com/Inna Sidorova
Editing by Laura Graves
Interior photographs by C. Nathan Pulley Photography

Llewellyn is a registered trademark of Llewellyn Worldwide Ltd.

Library of Congress Cataloging-in-Publication Data
Dow, Caroline.
  Tea leaf reading for beginners : your fortune in a teacup /
Caroline Dow. — 1st ed.
      p. cm.
  Includes bibliographical references.
  ISBN 978-0-7387-2329-7
  1. Fortune-telling by tea leaves. I. Title.
  BF1881.D69 2011
  133.3'244—dc22
                              2010046110

Llewellyn Publications
A Division of Llewellyn Worldwide Ltd.
2143 Wooddale Drive
Woodbury, MN 55125-2989
www.llewellyn.com

Printed in the United States of America

For Mother,
May your tea parties ever shine in the Summerland.

VERNA BEATRIZ WEIGOLT-GROVES

1922–2008

"Remember the tea kettle—it is always up to its neck in hot water, yet it still sings!"

—AUTHOR UNKNOWN

contents

acknowledgments

I would like to thank the following people: Sara Martinelli for her enthusiasm and encouragement throughout this project as well as for proofing the manuscript for accuracy of details about tea; Nathan Pulley for his stunning photography and the Dushanbe Teahouse for providing goodies for the photo shoot. Thanks also to Sue Wells for providing a valuable British perspective on the venerable custom of taking tea; Oscar Pimental, F & B Coordinator at Brown's Hotel for a truly unforgettable Afternoon Tea; and my husband John for treating me to Afternoon Teas around the world. Last, but certainly not least, I wish to thank my agent, Richard Curtis, for his efforts.

Part I

Tea Leaf Reading: An Age-Old Art for Today's World

*There is no trouble so great or grave
that cannot be much diminished
by a nice cup of tea.*

—BERNARD-PAUL HEROUX,
BASQUE PHILOSOPHER

Start reading someone's tea leaves at a party or in a restaurant, and I guarantee you'll soon draw a crowd. Everybody wants to know about the current influences on their lives and what the future holds. Tea leaf reading is an easily accessible, relatively uncomplicated and lighthearted way to take a stab at predicting the future. At the same time you can expand your circle of acquaintances and deepen friendships.

This mellow art benefits the teacup reader as much as the person for whom the leaves are read. Relaxing over a cup of tea provides quality time that otherwise tends to get consumed in the daily hustle-bustle. Practicing tea leaf divination forces you to slow your own hectic life pace along with that of your inquirer—the person having the reading. The enjoyment derived from the camaraderie of discussing life issues with friends and family can become as important as the actual divination.

The heyday of tea leaf reading occurred during Victorian times. With the invention of the teabag in 1908 and modern forms of entertainment such as television, videos, DVDs, and the Internet, the practice of this home-based art slid into steady decline. Now that children's wee tea parties, tea tastings for adults, and other tea-related leisure activities are making a comeback, tea leaf reading is riding a wave of renewed popularity.

This gentle pursuit of times gone by owes its regeneration, in part, to a nostalgic yearning for less complicated times. People are rediscovering that when they take time to brew and drink a cup of tea at the dining table—and perhaps serve accompanying little cakes and sandwiches—they encourage others to share their hopes, fears, accomplishments, and challenges. And a cup of tea costs pennies compared to a visit to a psychotherapist.

Another perk to tea leaf reading is that it acts as a self-development tool to enhance intuition and promote creative visualization. The images found in the teacup help focus your mind to explore inner worlds. By accessing symbols from your subconscious, you expand self-awareness.

Who Practices Tea Leaf Reading?

There was a time when most families boasted at least one amateur who interpreted everyone's leaves. When I was a girl, my great-aunt Lizzie enjoyed a peerless reputation as the family's resident psychic. On Sunday afternoons, she gathered us kids together in her kitchen around the lace-covered oak table to contemplate the depths of her delicate china cups. My aunt was not an educated woman. She never studied esoteric symbolism, and I doubt she ever heard of Jung or Freud. What she did possess was a keen intuitive mind and the ability to enchant us with the tales she told about what the future might bring. I feel lucky that she deigned to pass some of her knowledge along to me so that I, too, might read cups. It is difficult for me to imagine what my life would have been like without the enriching influence of tea leaf reading.

Looking back on the wisdom my auntie communicated, I realize that to be a successful tea leaf reader doesn't require graduate studies in arcane philosophy, as is the case with some tarot card readers. Nor need you meditate daily, as do many crystal ball gazers. Just follow the simple recipe Aunt Lizzie taught me that includes a tablespoonful of memorized symbols, a dollop of imagination, and a pinch of intuition, all presented with a storyteller's gift, and you're ready for action.

How Tea Leaf Reading Works

You may wonder how a bunch of lowly wet leaves left in the dregs of a teacup can show a person's future. Is it an old wives' tale spawned on superstition? Some of the mystery surrounding tea leaf reading can be attributed to the reader's largely unconscious capacity to interpret minute bits of information transmitted by the inquirer. Such data might include nonverbal behaviors like posture, facial expressions, eye movements, and hand gestures. The way a person dresses and an accent and speech pattern also reveal information.

Yet there is more to the accuracy of tea leaf predictions than what meets the eye. After all, this type of divination has been practiced for centuries with good enough results that people from diverse cultures around the world continue to practice it. So what's the secret?

The fact is, seasoned psychics, and even I, you, my neighbor down the block, and a stranger from another town all possess some knowledge of the future. It's because we are interconnected with each other and to the cosmos. Think of *Six Degrees of Separation,* only on the mental plane, and you get an idea of what I mean. Some attribute this interconnectedness to a theory rooted in a relatively new science called quantum physics.

According to researchers in this field, everything that exists is interconnected. On a cellular level, each cell in our bodies contains all the past, present, and future information about us. When we touch an object, our brains use a subtle form of energy to transmit our data through our bodies to the object, where it gets lodged. Some items make better recorders of this energy than others. Small objects like tea leaves, coffee grounds, seeds, and even pebbles seem particularly impressionable.

In the case of tea leaves, they reveal the stored information by clinging together on the sides and bottom of the cup after the tea is drunk. The inquirer subconsciously impregnates the leaves with the information. The leaves then arrange themselves into images that the reader can interpret using his or her connectedness to the cup and to the inquirer. Such pictures can be construed either literally or symbolically as snapshots of the inquirer's life.

Given the fact that everything is interrelated, you might ask yourself the same question that Scrooge put to the Ghost of Christmas Future in Charles Dickens' classic tale *A Christmas Carol*: "Are these images of what will happen, or of what might happen?"

Psychologists remind us that past behavior is usually the best predictor of future behavior. Images formed by the leaves give a good idea of what is likely to occur if the inquirer follows typical behavior patterns. When the predicted outcome is unsatisfactory, the person can always do something to break the chain of events and change the future. In other words, forewarned is forearmed. This is why people go for readings of any kind, from astrology charts to tarot.

Presumably, along with a fresh cup of tea, the reader also brings to the table a fresh eye, free from prejudice. In this way, the most accurate interpretation can be made of what is likely to occur, and the inquirer's available resources to deal with the situation can be identified.

I trust that in a very good way, you will get more than you bargained for from reading these pages. First of all, I hope you discover the joys of tea leaf reading for yourself, friends, and family. You'll learn everything from choosing the right tea to answering your best friend's question about whether that longed-for soul mate is ever going to put in an appearance. By the time you finish reading this book, you will know how to prepare the cup, decipher images, and make predictions that will astound everyone—including yourself—with their accuracy. Besides interpreting the leaves, you will get ideas on how to throw a fabulous tea leaf reading party and other kinds of tea events. And you will be able to entertain your guests and inquirers with yarns about the history of tea and humorous tea superstitions that have come down to us over the ages. You will even learn twenty ways to use tea besides drinking it and how to cook with tea.

Sherlock Holmes' favorite tea was Lapsang Souchong. In the spirit of detection that he represents, I have just prepared myself a cup of this smoky brew. With teacup in hand, I invite you to settle back in a comfortable reading chair and turn the page as I unravel for you the mysteries of tea leaf reading and more.

one

Before You Begin

*The best quality tea must have creases like the
leathern boot of Tartar horsemen, curl like the
dewlap of a mighty bullock, unfold like a mist
rising out of a ravine, gleam like a lake touched
by a zephyr, and be wet and soft like a fine
earth newly swept by rain.*

—LU YU, AUTHOR OF *THE CLASSIC ON TEA*,
THE FIRST BOOK ON TEA

The above may have been true for Lu Yu, but I prefer a sweetly scented jasmine green so I can incorporate the flowery residue into my readings. But I digress.

Okay, you want to be a tea leaf reader for fun, for profit—if the laws of your state permit—or in a sincere desire to help people achieve their highest potentials. How do you start? It's really not very complicated. All you need besides tea is a teacup, hot water, and—of course—your intuition. Other useful additions include a saucer, spoon, napkin, and perhaps a dictionary of symbols such as the one found in Part II of this book.

Teacups

An actual teacup—not a mug or a Styrofoam cup—seems to work best for most people. If you don't already own one, you can pick up a relatively inexpensive cup at a junk store, antiques emporium, or online. Proper teacups, like the delicate ones my great-aunt drank from, are wider at the top than at the base. This shape helps the leaves settle around the sides of the cup in easily decipherable patterns. Cups with high vertical sides, small openings at the top, or undulating patterns around the inside cause the leaves to bunch up, making them difficult to interpret. Not to mention the superstition that leaves piled high on the side of the cup foretell misfortune. If opposite the handle, the trouble emanates from outside forces; if around the handle, the inquirer has only him- or herself to blame.

Plain, unadorned cups are simplest to read, especially for beginners. Although any color will do, transparent cups or ones with designs on the inside are not practical, as they can distract the reader and distort impressions. For me, the perfect cup is fashioned from white porcelain and slopes gently outward from the base. Some readers prefer square cups because they pinpoint events using the corners as a frame of reference. Unfortunately, square cups are hard to find, plus, at least for me, the leaves tend to stick together at the corners in blobs. And blobs, as you will find in Part II, are signs of confused thinking. And who wants to be confused?

Saucers

Saucers make a practical addition because they hold the cup, a spoon, and a perhaps a wedge of lemon. In tasseomancy—a fancy term for tea leaf reading—the saucer also captures the spilled tea when the inquirer inverts the cup for the reading. (You'll learn more about how to invert the cup in the next chapter.) Teacups are usually sold with saucers, but nothing written in the leaves says that cups and saucers have to match. In fact, mismatched sets can make a chic decorating statement, so don't be concerned about this detail if you buy your china secondhand.

Once during a tasseomancy workshop, a student asked me, "What if all the leaves fall out?" With a laugh I assured her, "It never happens." When the woman turned her cup upside down—you guessed it—all the leaves came dribbling out. I read her saucer and used her physical position across from me to substitute for the cup's handle to pinpoint events in time. I'll talk more about timing events later.

I've always known that coffee-ground interpreters read the saucer, but since the incident with my student, I've met a couple of readers who actually prefer to interpret the saucer instead of the cup. They ask the inquirer to drink the tea, and then invert the dregs onto the saucer, gently tapping out all the leaves. Before reading, the interpreter dabs away the excess teaspoonful of spilled liquid with the corner of a napkin, taking care not to disturb the leaves. This idea sounded so exciting to me that I've started incorporating saucer reading into my own interpretations, with good results.

Accessories: Spoon, Napkin

The last two recommended pieces of equipment are the napkin and spoon. Instruct your inquirer before drinking to stir the full cup clockwise three times to distribute the leaves evenly. Place the napkin between the cup and saucer to absorb spills before inverting the cup.

After the inquirer inverts the cup and you begin to interpret the symbols, use the narrow end of the spoon to pinpoint the images you find. Pointing at the symbols helps the inquirer visualize the pictures and understand that they are not figments of the imagination. Using the back of a spoon also helps keep delicate images intact. Nothing is more disconcerting than to jab at a symbol with a clumsy finger and watch it disintegrate before your eyes. Believe it or not, learning to consistently use the spoon is the single most difficult detail for beginning tea leaf readers to master.

Tea: Plant of Heaven

If you're determined to read tea leaves, you're going to have to drink some tea—such a sacrifice! So it's probably a good idea to become informed about different kinds of tea, and then learn which ones to use for different types of readings. If you're eager to start reading, skip the rest of this chapter and go on to chapter 2. You can always come back and find out more about tea later.

What's in This Strange Brew?

If you think your favorite chamomile, rooibos, or yerba maté blend is a tea, you are mistaken—at least technically. Even though they are popularly known as teas, these are really herbal tisanes or infusions. I take up herbal beverages in chapter 5. All real tea comes from a kind of camellia, the *Thea sinensis.* This flowering evergreen shrub, when left without pruning, grows into a tree. Tea growers prune shrubs to facilitate leaf harvesting. The tea shrub thrives at high altitudes in humid climates near the equator.

Although the plant likes heat and lots of rainfall, it grows best when the leaves are shaded from the searing sun.

Although tea originated in China, currently only around three percent of the production for international markets is grown there. Today India and Sri Lanka are substantial producers. Nevertheless, tea is harvested in such diverse places as Japan, Mozambique, Papua/New Guinea, the Democratic Republic of the Congo, and Guatemala. In blending, India teas are selected for strength, Ceylon for flavor, and African varieties for color. China teas blend especially well with Ceylon and Darjeeling, the latter of which is also known as "the champagne of teas."

Teas are categorized as green, white, oolong, and black. Their categorization refers to the length of time leaves ferment before drying in a process known as oxidation. Oxidation adds spice and aroma to the leaves.

Steamed leaves, rolled quickly and dried before oxidation sets in, are called green teas. Lately, green tea has been touted as a health potion to regularize systemic imbalances, help promote weight loss, stimulate hair growth, and cut cholesterol. Some people even claim that unfermented leaves, when drunk, slow aging. Clearly these enthusiasts consider green tea a veritable panacea. Green teas are ranked according to leaf age, style, and size, with the best quality coming from lightly rolled, early leaf buds and leaves.

White teas are a kind of green tea where only the unopened buds and youngest leaves are picked. They undergo the identical process in the same way as green teas, only even more quickly to ensure that no oxidation occurs. Brewed white teas are light-colored and emit a delicate, grassy aroma.

Semi-oxidized leaves make the subtle-flavored oolong teas. Tea masters grade them according to quality and taste. It seems a shame that more people don't know about these fragrant, flavorful teas. I, for one, would like to see them become more widely available.

Fully oxidized leaves create the more full-bodied familiar black teas we find in most restaurants and drink iced. Black teas are graded according to leaf size and appearance. Whether leaves are whole or broken does not indicate quality. The grading system is complicated and falls outside the scope of this book. Suffice it to say that the capital letters you often find printed on labels of tins and boxes of tea, such as BOP and SFTGOFOP, refer to tea grades. For those of you who wish to know more about the intricacies of grading tea, I include some definitions in the glossary.

The very smallest leaves and tiniest broken bits left over from the manufacturing process are called

fannings and dust. The term "dust" sounds unappetizing, I know. But I can assure you that the manufacturers don't scoop dust from the factory floor,
and that many of these smallest leaves can be quite
palatable. In fact, if you drink teabag tea, you have
been enjoying fannings and dust without knowing
it; many manufacturers reserve these small pieces for
their teabags.

As far as tea leaf reading is concerned, teabags are
considered a no-no. Most tea leaf readers find that
teabag tea is too powdery to form clear images in the
cup. Even though I am sure purists will balk, if you
find yourself in a pinch, I suggest you flout conven-
tion and break open that teabag to read the dregs.
In my opinion, reading from a split teabag is better
than performing no reading at all. Anyway, I believe
the images that form in the cup have more to do
with the person drinking the tea and the interpreter
than with the leaves themselves.

For example, I remember once during a trans-
atlantic flight to London a young woman was des-
perate for me to give her a reading. Luckily, we were
traveling on a British airliner. Although they only
supplied teabags on this flight, we were able to bor-
row a proper teacup from first class. I opened a bag
and gave the girl a reading that highlighted her current love interest in Scotland, the reason for her trip.
I identified a heart and a ring in close proximity, fol-

lowed by a church steeple on the far side of the cup. It all pointed to the probability that the fellow would pop the question soon and that they would tie the knot a few months thereafter. I was glad I used the teabag because I was able to allay the young woman's concerns.

Although I didn't photograph that particular teacup, here is a photo of a cup read from teabag leaves:

Note that the leaves look quite powdery. Nonetheless, at least one recognizable symbol emerges, the image of a shirt. It also looks like the arm and hand attached to the shirt is holding a club. Shirts stand for protection. So in this cup, I would say that either the inquirer is a protector of smaller, weaker people and animals or that the inquirer is being protected from some annoying situation or problem. The meaning I would choose would depend on the other images found in the cup.

Scented Teas

The teas we drink sometimes are blended or scented. Some people mistakenly think that Orange Pekoe (pronounced "*peck*-oh") is a type of scented tea. The term actually refers to a large-leaf tea that, when first introduced to the West, was marketed as the preferred tea of the Dutch royal House of Orange. Jasmine tea, a favorite in many Chinese restaurants, is an example of a tea scented with jasmine flowers. To create scented teas, growers may add blossoms during the drying process. After the tea passes through the final drying stage, the crisp flowers are removed, leaving a delicate fragrance and flavor. Other manufacturers may scent teas with essential oils. Always read the label to make sure the tea has been scented with essential oils, not with synthetics. Synthetics can be harmful if ingested.

A veritable potpourri of botanicals can be used to scent teas. Some common choices include bergamot, chamomile, chrysanthemum, cinnamon, clove buds, fennel, gardenia, ginger, hibiscus, jasmine, lavender, lime, lychee, marigold, narcissus, nutmeg, orange, peach tree leaves, rose, saffron, vanilla bean, and violet. Constant Comment, a popular blend based on an antebellum Southern recipe, relies on peels and spices to create its distinctive flavor.

Traditionalists claim you should never adulterate the leaves you use for a reading with flowers, herbs, peels, or spices. They make a sour face at the mere mention of adding lemon, with its messy pulp and occasional seed. Others, like me, are fond of incorporating into their readings the images that botanicals form. Besides, I find that some clients who refuse to touch black tea can be persuaded to try an herbal infusion. Many herbs carry their own traditional meanings, such as peppermint for money, chamomile for success, and rose for love, just for starters. Sometimes I offer these infusions or black teas scented with botanicals for theme readings.

Choosing the Right Tea

Of all these varieties, which are the best for tea leaf reading? Loose-leaf teas—black, oolong, green, white, or herbal infusions—work equally well, but you may want to vary the tea according to the kind of reading you want to perform.

Coarse teas like Gunpowder Green and many herbal blends tend to produce a few bold images, which make them ideal choices for short readings. I once performed a sample reading for a newspaper photographer who was taking pictures for an article on tea leaf reading. During the shoot, he drank a cup of chamomile tea.

A few large flowers left on the side of the cup clung together to form what looked like a single perfect tree or perhaps an arrow pointing upward. This made a clear image for the photo shoot. It boded well for the photographer, too. Trees stand for fulfilled wishes, changes for the better, good health, and endurance. Arrows indicate a message or direction to follow. Suffice it to say, the photographer soon moved onward and upward from that small local paper to work at a national newspaper.

Finer teas like China Black and Ceylon render more numerous, complex designs that often show one large figure and several smaller groupings. Such images are appropriate for an inquirer with many questions or a busy lifestyle, or one who requests a general reading. Interestingly, the same tea will produce diverse picture styles for different people.

No matter the kind of tea you choose, it can go stale over time. To preserve freshness, store your teas in airtight containers and away from direct sunlight, and never in the refrigerator. Sara Martinelli, tea master of the renowned Dushanbe Teahouse in Boulder, Colorado, recommends keeping green teas for no longer than three to six months, oolongs for six to nine months, and black teas for no more than one year. If your tea goes stale sooner and you wish to revive it, spread a thin layer of it on a sheet of paper for a few hours in a well-aired room. If that doesn't work, chapter 7 offers some non-beverage uses for tea.

Ten Teas for Ten Readings

Following are ten of my favorite teas and blends for readings.

1. **Earl Grey**—You can count on this fine-leafed black tea scented with bergamot to hit the spot with most people. Even those who don't normally drink tea often tolerate it well. Since the leaves produce many detailed images, Earl Grey makes a terrific tea for a general or year-long reading.

2. **Gunpowder Green**—Despite its rather daunting name derived from the dried leaves' similar appearance to gunpowder pellets, this is a delicately flavored tea. It produces a few bold shapes, which makes it ideal for a quick or one-question reading.

3. **Chamomile**—The sunny yellow flowers are associated with good health, wealth, and

success. Chamomile makes a fine tea for questions relating to career, business, projects, and medical conditions. As an added benefit, it quells digestive problems and helps you sleep.

4. **Black** tea scented with jasmine, rose, or hibiscus petals—These tasty teas are just right for questions involving love, romance, and friendship.

5. **Peppermint** or **Spearmint**—Either tea can be used for questions relating to prosperity, money, real estate, or inheritance issues.

6. **White Peony**—I recommend this mild but deliciously refreshing tea for questions concerning matters of spirit. Many who find black teas too strong tolerate it well.

7. **Blend for New Beginnings**—From time to time, my clients request readings about new projects, changes of residence, or fresh starts. For such inquiries, I whip up a mixture of Ceylon black tea and add pinches of ginger root, nettles, and ginseng for renewed strength and energy.

8. **Constant Comment**—Almost everybody in the family will like the spicy taste of Constant Comment, so it makes an excellent choice for questions centered on home, family, and

relationships. After it steeps, this tea appears orange-colored in the cup. In the language of color, orange is the mental version of that well-known mascot bunny who sells batteries. According to color psychology theory, this hue helps clear and revitalize the intellect. Offer it for readings about increasing willpower or adaptation to changing circumstances, as well as for queries concerning intellectual pursuits.

9. **Tea for the Coffee Lover**—If an inveterate coffee drinker who cannot abide the thought of quaffing a cup of that nasty "tea stuff" comes to you for a reading, you have two choices: You can break down and prepare a cup of coffee and read the grounds or, better yet, ask the inquirer to drink a cup of tea made from the following ingredients: ¾ teaspoon roasted chicory root and ¼ teaspoon roasted dandelion root. The flavor of this herbal infusion is close to the taste of coffee, only it doesn't contain the caffeine. Some coffee drinkers also find the strong taste of the brewed herb yerba maté a reasonable substitution.

10. **Spirited Tea**—If you want to read your own cup and enhance your intuitive abilities in the bargain, try this blend. Take ½ teaspoon

of any green tea you like and add a sprinkling of lemon peel and pinches of lemon balm, dandelion leaf, blackberry leaf, and three or four anise seeds. All are alleged to open the psychic centers not to mention tickle your taste buds. Yum!

Zodiac Teas

If you know your inquirer's birth sign, you might want to experiment with a zodiac tea. You will need to make these blends in advance as they require several ingredients, but how to store twelve different blends, at most? Our household consumes a lot of olives, so after I run an empty glass container through the dishwasher, I put together enough individual zodiac blends to fill the eight-ounce jar. Then I label and store the container in the cabinet where I keep my other teas. If I haven't used it up after six months, I fertilize my azaleas with the contents, and whip up a fresh batch.

Every botanical is associated with an astrological sign or one of the planets in our solar system. This tradition dates back to medieval times and is based on many things, including the color and appearance of the plant and empirical testing for what kinds of ailments the botanicals appeared to cure. In those days, doctors and herbalists believed people had propensities toward certain diseases according to the parts of the body their signs ruled.

Although science has never proved any of this to be true, plenty of anecdotal evidence recorded over time and in diverse cultures helps support the theory. For example, Virgos are said to suffer from intestinal ailments; therefore fennel is recommended for them. Boneset is alleged to help cure Capricorns' bone problems.

My blends consist of botanicals associated with their corresponding zodiac signs. In order to help maintain balance, I also include something from the sign's opposite number; that is the sign directly across the wheel of the zodiac, six signs away. For example, in the Aries formula, I put in a pinch of watercress, an herb governed by Libra. Scorpio's formula contains some lovage, a Taurus botanical. The following recipes do not give exact amounts; each reader will probably want to concoct a different ratio according to taste. Larger amounts are listed first, and you can expect to add only a pinch or two of the last botanicals listed. I recommend you experiment to find which flavors please you most. For more information on zodiac teas and astrology, turn to chapter 27.

Aries
Orange Pekoe tea, nettles, peppermint, red clover, hawthorn berries, golden seal, watercress

Taurus
Oolong tea, dandelion leaves, lovage, dandelion root, horehound, licorice root

Gemini
Black tea scented with roses, lavender buds, queen of the meadow, vervain, caraway seeds, hops

Cancer
White Peony tea, lemongrass, lemon balm, honeysuckle flowers, violet leaves, boneset

Leo
Rooibos tea, blackberry leaf, angelica root, linden flowers and bracts, star anise

Virgo
Lemon-scented green tea, blueberry tea, skullcap, rosehips, fennel seeds, jasmine flowers

Libra
Lady Grey tea (I like the Twinings and Tazo brands), strawberry leaves, watercress, violet flowers, marjoram

Scorpio
Gunpowder green tea, Solomon's seal, raspberry leaves, orange peel, grains of paradise, lovage

Sagittarius
Earl Grey tea, wild cherry bark, wood betony, hawthorn berries, lavender buds

Capricorn
Russian Caravan tea, peppermint, boneset, hyssop, lemon balm

Aquarius
Darjeeling tea, eyebright, spikenard, strawberry leaves, aniseed

Pisces
China tea, elder flowers, hibiscus flowers, ginger root, Irish moss, chamomile

The foregoing suggested blends show the kinds of teas that work well for me. Even if neither you nor your inquirer does not believe in astrology, these blends are fun to try as a novelty. Naturally, you may choose any kind of tea you or your inquirer would like, and it's fun to concoct your own blends.

———

Now that you know how to put together the dry ingredients, it's time to turn the page and find out how to brew the perfect cup of tea for tea leaf reading.

two

Getting Started

You've hustled around putting together your teas.
Next comes the easy part—finding someone
who will let you read the leaves. And who better to
start with than the most fascinating person you'll
probably ever read for? I'm talking about yourself,
of course!

Reading for Number One

Admit it—you're curious about what the future holds
for you, or you wouldn't be interested in divination.

You are a captive audience, and the more you practice on Number One, the better you'll get at interpreting the leaves, both for yourself and for others. I try to read my cup each morning to center myself, activate my intuitive brain, and foresee what surprises the day may have in store. I also read my own cup whenever I have a burning question, which is almost every day.

I suggest you keep a personal tea leaf reading diary where you note the symbols that appear and reappear, the ways in which you decode them, and how many of your prophecies come true. You'll shed light on your own life patterns and come to understand your unique explanations for various symbols.

Because you are invested in yourself, you may misinterpret some symbols as wish fulfillments or dreaded fears. For example, once I saw in my cup what at first glance looked like a horse's head. This symbol signifies the advent of an ardent lover. "Hmm, intriguing," I thought. But when I stared at the image for a minute, it started to look more like a bull's head, a sign of stubbornness. Not so fascinating! Naturally, I ignored the bull and went for the horse's head. I told myself I was going with my first impressions like I'm supposed to do. It didn't have anything to do with wish fulfillment—nothing at all. Much to my chagrin, two days later, somebody with a big ego, acting like a bull in a tea room, charged into my life and wreaked major havoc. Sometimes it's hard to be honest with yourself, especially if you ardently desire something. For this reason, many psychics occasionally go to other readers.

Preparing to Read the Leaves

To avoid misinterpreting symbols and to dip down into your subconscious mind, which links both you and your inquirer to the cosmos, it helps to balance yourself before starting a reading. Take a few slow, deep breaths and silently request guidance from God, the universe, your Guardian Angel, or any deity or force in which you believe. If you wish, light candles or incense, anoint yourself with any good psychic visioning oil, surround yourself with crystals, play heavenly background music, or perform your readings in a room decorated in a special way. Do whatever helps put you in a relaxed (but alert) state of mind. Many readers follow the same procedures they would if they were meditating.

Reading for Others

People have their tea leaves read for many reasons. Some brim with questions about love, money, legal or business issues, incidents at work, children, family, or health. Others seek direction for spiritual growth. Then there are those with no particular agenda, who come to satisfy their curiosity.

No matter their questions, it helps for you to focus their attention and yours by asking them why they want a reading. Those who malign psychics will probably accuse you of cheating. So what? You know that when you ask your inquirer for information, you're not trying to fake out anyone. You are making it easier for them to subconsciously instill their cups with information they need to know. Focusing on their question also helps guide you toward making the best interpretation. A symbol can have multiple meanings. If you know in advance your inquirers' issues, you can choose the most appropriate meanings for their special situations.

Interpretation Duet

Let me give you an analogy. My husband and I take piano lessons together. Because I am more experienced, when recital time rolls around and we have to play a duet, our teacher usually gives me the more difficult part to play. My husband interprets the easier sections, and his bass notes enhance the notes of my treble sections. Together we make a reasonably solid, well-executed-sounding whole. In tea leaf reading, you have more experience and practice reading symbols than your inquirer. That person, while new to the game, has more knowledge and experience with his or her own life.

Two Heads and All That Jazz

Here's an example. Once I saw in a cup a gigantic shark, teeth bared, bearing down on a toddler and infant. In tea leaf reading language, sharks can symbolize lawyers, and babies can stand for new projects or worries. I mentioned this and asked my inquirer if she had any lawsuits pending over two issues, one being more significant (larger) than the other.

Instantly, she knew what the reading was about. The problem had nothing to do with a lawsuit, but with a barracuda of a boss who sharply criticized her and a coworker for no good reason and threatened to fire them if they didn't straighten up. The toddler represented the inquirer, and the coworker, less important in the inquirer's eyes, was the baby. Further on in the cup, I spotted two people standing together under a lovely palm tree with the sun shining in the background. I told the inquirer that I thought the boss would soon be moving on and that she and her coworker would receive a rich reward for their suffering. Two months later, my inquirer called me to confirm that her boss left the firm and upper management had rewarded her and the coworker with paid vacations for a project they had successfully completed.

Topical Tea

Another reason to know the purpose of the reading is to select an appropriate tea for the topic. Simple yes/no questions are best answered with a coarse tea that renders a few bold images. White teas are good for shedding light on spiritual matters. Your inquirer may even request a "past time" reading. In this instance, the person has questions about how previous actions have influenced present circumstances, or wants to learn about a past life. A fitting tea for such a reading is a small-leafed China Black scented with jasmine or lotus blossoms. As time considerations are not an issue in a past time reading, you need not take into account the positions where the leaves fall with relation to the handle. In fact, you may wish to dispense with the cup entirely and read the saucer.

Be Observant

Whatever your inquirers' motivations, observe their body language and behavior. If anyone appears timid or anxious, you will want to couch your reading in even more tactful terms than you would normally. If the inquirer acts standoffish or even rude, you can assume the person came to test your skills. Even those who play at "fool the psychic" are often drawn to visit a reader out of a subconscious need to clarify an issue or explore concerns. Often the leaves will startle them by coming up with information that will have a potentially decisive impact on their lives.

Whatever the purpose for the reading, unexpected information may arise. Always consider the inquirer's stated question first, but do not hesitate to add extra bits of data as the reading progresses. After all, the inquirer may have wanted a reading for one reason on a conscious level, but subconsciously hopes for responses to an entirely different dilemma.

Answering Yes/No Questions

While the tea leaves can cast light on specific questions, they are not as adept at yes/no answers as other divinatory methods, such as the pendulum or the Ouija board. Those methods are designed to answer in the affirmative or negative to an inquiry, and not much else. If your client has a specific query, select an herbal infusion or a coarse tea like Gunpowder Green. When placing hands over the cup, encourage your guest to concentrate on the question from all possible angles to give the truest reading. An example of this is in a sample reading in chapter 4.

Reading for an Absent Inquirer

If necessary, you can read a cup for someone who is not physically present. I have done this many times through my mail-order business for clients who live around the world and cannot come to me. Prepare the tea as if you were drinking it for yourself. As you sit to drink, set before you a photo of the inquirer, or if you don't have one, a piece of paper with the person's name, geographical location, birth date, and questions written, if possible, in the individual's handwriting. It is hypothesized that such divinations are possible because every cell in our bodies contains a hologram of the entire universe. The hologram, in turn, connects you to the inquirer. For that brief period when you are drinking the tea, you become, in essence, the person for whom you are reading.

"How Often Should I Read?"

This question almost always surfaces in my workshops. Fledgling readers are concerned about "upsetting the spirits" with their queries. Or they worry that they will overindulge, and therefore, no useful information will emerge.

I believe you can read for yourself as often as you want, even once a day. In fact, I encourage it. By putting yourself through your tea leaf reading paces daily, you hone your intuitive mind and keep it singing like a steaming teakettle. When you need to marshal your skills to aid your inquirer, both you and your intuition will be ready. Although some may think it excessive to do personal readings on a daily basis, consider that the process helps you better understand yourself. When you know yourself well, you become a strong, centered individual in a good position to help others. You also acquire a deeper understanding of your personal symbol meanings.

Reading for others is another matter. People can get hooked on visiting psychics, especially if the reader is often on target. Spiritual readers function in many ways like psychologists and counselors. As can happen with any professional in those fields, clients may come to rely on you for advice about every little thing rather than work on coming up with solutions for their own problems. Again, in such cases I advise you to use your intuition. Each person's life moves at a different rhythm and pace. Some in high-pressure jobs or with too much on their plates may run around like radio-operated toy cars on steroids. Such inquirers probably could benefit from frequent readings, if for no other reason than it forces them to take a time-out for an hour and contemplate their lives. Others who lead more placid, bucolic existences may not face changes in their situations for many months. Everything depends on individuals and your intuitive feelings toward them.

Brewing the Perfect Cup

By now, you've reeled in a willing guinea pig—that is, an inquirer who doesn't mind you practicing—and you are set to brew that fateful cup of tea. One of the best ways to enjoy a good cup of tea for nourishment or pleasure is to prepare an infusion. If you are drinking tea for pleasure, boil one cupful of water, pour it into a warmed cup over one teaspoonful of leaves, and steep for up to five minutes. If you brew it in a pot, use a nonmetal receptacle. Add an extra teaspoonful "for the pot," as the British say.

If you use a pot, fill it with hot water. Once the pot is warmed, empty the water down the drain, spoon in the tea, and pour boiling water over the leaves. Strain out the leaves if you are not planning to perform a tea leaf reading, and pour the brewed beverage into a teacup. Again, if you don't intend to do a reading from the cup, you can add sugar, honey or molasses, milk, or lemon. Stir to dissolve any additions, and drink while hot. Natural soft, filtered water makes a superior cup of tea.

Brewing for Tea Leaf Reading

To read someone's leaves, you can either brew a pot of tea or prepare a single cupful. If you are reading for more than one person, or decide to drink a companionable cuppa along with your inquirer, a full pot is the way to go. Simply spoon ½ teaspoon of leaves into the bottom of your inquirer's cup before pouring strained tea from the pot.

Also use only half a teaspoon of leaves for a single cup when you want to pour boiling water instead of tea over the leaves. Some of my workshop participants at first put in too many leaves. They don't realize how much leaves swell when brewed. Too many leaves translate into blobs on the side of the cup. Blobs are difficult to decipher and, as I've mentioned elsewhere, are considered a sign of confused thinking—bad news when you think about it.

Do not strain the leaves or add sweetener or milk when preparing a cup for a reading. These substances make for sticky leaves that make messy clumps on the sides of the cup. On the other hand, a squeezed wedge of lemon is fine, if the inquirer wants it. As I have mentioned elsewhere, any seed or piece of pulp left in the cup after it is drunk can be incorporated into the reading.

If you have a faucet that automatically dispenses hot water, use it as a quick method to prepare a single cup. The only fast preparation method I discourage is using the microwave oven to heat the water. Tea brewed that way tastes flat, and besides, it's not traditional—tea leaf reading is all about tradition.

Now place the napkin on top of the saucer, and the full cup of tea on top of the napkin. Let the tea steep for three to five minutes. Brewing the tea enhances the flavor and lets the leaves fatten so they create easily decipherable patterns. When the tea has steeped, ask your inquirer to stir the cup once to evenly distribute the leaves.

First Step in Divination

It's time to perform a preliminary examination of the cup. Keep a spoon close by so you can point with the handle at any formations you see. Scan the surface of the water.

- Bubbles mean a monetary windfall.

- Sticks or stray leaves floating on top of the water foretell visitations; a short or thin stick stands for a woman, a long or stout one represents a man.

- A single leaf floating on top of the water predicts money streaming the inquirer's way; many floating leaves do not foretell a windfall—they simply nullify the original meaning.

- A leaf stuck at the rim of the cup means an influential person will soon enter the inquirer's life: if the leaf is near the handle, the stranger lives nearby; if on the side of the cup opposite the handle, the person will travel from some distance—maybe even from abroad.

Tell your inquirer to place his or her hands over the cup, make a wish, and leisurely drink all but one teaspoonful (a small sip) of the liquid.

Inverting the Cup:
Slow and Fast Inversion Methods

Next, instruct your inquirer to gently rotate the cup, sloshing around the liquid in a counterclockwise direction, using the left hand. The left is the intuitive hand, which represents the right brain and subconscious mind. Ask your client to take the cup in both hands and tip it slowly, rotating it all the while until the teaspoonful of tea trickles out evenly and the cup is inverted over the napkin covering the saucer. Have the person set the cup upside down on top of the napkin to let it drain.

This slow inversion method is a bit tricky, and some people may feel clumsy or perhaps unable to overcome their aversion to making a mess. In this case, tell the person that the napkin will absorb the spill. Let your inquirer swirl the liquid around the cup and invert it over the napkin all at once. Then ask your client to set the cup upside down on the napkin and turn it clockwise three times to evenly distribute the leaves. Your inquirer can also simply slosh the liquid around and slowly invert the cup without twirling it.

No matter which inversion method the inquirer chooses, some leaves inevitably are lost. If all the leaves fall out, you can always read the saucer. Remember you are asking your inquirers to go through these inversion acrobatics so the leaves will pick up impressions from their auras and arrange themselves to reflect their current life situations.

By tradition, any liquid left in the cup after it has been inverted and left to drain for a few minutes foretells tears to be shed. So when you turn the cup right-side up and prepare to read, be sure to dab away any remaining liquid with a corner of a napkin. It is said that if liquid still remains, the trouble in the inquirer's life will persist. If the liquid changes the formations of the leaves, so will the inquirer's life be afflicted by disappointment. Of course, it could also mean the inquirer did a messy job inverting the cup!

Here's a summary of what you've learned so far about preparing the cup for tea leaf reading. Use it as a quick reference.

Preparations at a Glance

1. Choose, brew, and pour the tea.
2. Set out the saucer, napkin, cup, and spoon.
3. Relax and make a wish.
4. Stir the leaves.
5. Scan the surface for divination.

6. Drink all but one teaspoonful.

7. Swirl the leaves, invert the cup, and drain.

Iced Tea Readings

If, during the sweltering summertime, you can't stand the thought of drinking tea hot, do the following. Brew the hot tea and instead of adding ice cubes, chill the liquid in the refrigerator along with some leaves from the pot. When you are ready to read, awaken the leaves by stirring them. Better yet, let your inquirer stir. Then without using a strainer, pour the cold liquid into a teacup for your inquirer to drink. If enough leaves don't flow into the cup to perform a satisfactory reading, add an additional ½ teaspoon of leftover brewed leaves.

———

Ready for the moment of truth? Turn the page and discover the secrets of how to understand the past and present and foretell the future reading tea leaves.

three

Time to Interpret

*Find yourself a cup of tea; the teapot is behind
you. Now tell me about hundreds of things.*

—SAKI, EDWARDIAN-ERA SHORT-STORY
AUTHOR AND PLAYWRIGHT

At last you are ready to examine the leaves. Turn the cup upright and use the edge of a napkin to dab away any remaining liquid. From a practical standpoint, you'll want to have all the liquid out of the cup so the leaves don't shift during the reading.

Take a look at the patterns the leaves have formed on the inside of the cup. Relax and take your time. If you need to focus, take a few deep breaths. If it helps, pretend you're lying on your back on a grassy knoll in the springtime. Imagine pictures are taking shape like they do in the cloud formations floating by in the sky. Or perhaps you prefer to visualize conjuring up images from a crackling fire in the hearth or campfire. Never force an image because you feel under pressure to see something for your inquirer. You don't want to inject "left brain," rationalized thoughts into the reading. Let the pictures flow from your subconscious into your conscious mind like tea poured from the pot into a cup. Examine the cup from all angles. You even can turn it upside down, as long as you are careful not to disturb the leaves. Trust your first impressions, and don't overanalyze.

Tea Leaf Reading in Six Easy Steps

It took seven steps to prepare the cup, so the following mere six steps to interpretation should be a piece of (tea) cake for you.

1. First, look for concrete, realistic shapes such as faces, people, animals, trees and flowers, and familiar objects like vehicles, dwellings, furniture, household equipment, clothing, and jewelry. Such symbols hold specific meanings in tea leaf reading. For example, trees and flowers usually mean success, fulfillment, and happiness. The symbolism chapters in Part II give the meanings for many common objects.

2. Next, scan the cup for geometrical forms, including triangles, circles, ovals, squares, dots, and lines. For example, a dot that appears near a symbol enhances its meaning.

3. Go on to numbers, letters, and spelled-out words. Yes, you will occasionally find entire words and sometimes even phrases spelled in the cup. I've even seen words written in Portuguese, my second language.

   Once, I clearly distinguished in a cup the word "moving." When I asked the inquirer if she was planning to change residences, her face turned cherry-red and she demanded to know who told me she was moving to nearby Fort Collins in three days. I had to point to the word with the back of my spoon to convince her that the humble leaves had unmasked her closely guarded secret. Numbers usually stand for some kind of time frame, such as two days, three weeks, or four months. Letters often— but not always—refer to the initials of people who will play important roles in the inquirer's future.

4. Note common universal symbols like crosses, stars, zodiac signs, and playing card suits. Again, refer to Part II for a list of symbols and their interpretations. To increase your

knowledge beyond the meanings offered in this book, you may want to invest in a symbols dictionary. *A Dictionary of Symbols* by J. E. Cirlot is one such book. Migene González-Wippler's *Dreams and What They Mean to You* (St. Paul, MN: Llewellyn, 2002), also deciphers symbolic meanings. Remember to keep a record of your personal interpretations, which are equally important as textbook definitions.

In tea leaf reading—as in many of the other "-mantic" arts, that is, divination—you can get bogged down trying to stick to fixed symbol definitions. If you are inflexible on this point, your reading can quickly turn pedantic-sounding, or worse, nonsensical. On the other hand, you may not always agree with standard definitions. For example, many symbols dictionaries associate bats with false friends and treachery. But I usually interpret a bat as a protection sign—like Batman. For the Chinese, the bat is a harbinger of long life and good luck. Always go with your intuition when offering an interpretation.

Recently, I saw two lovers in a cup. None of the other symbols seemed to be associated with romance; they all had to do with business. So I went for a less common meaning for this symbol and told the inquirer that a choice was being offered to him at work. The leaves indicated that he would make a decision that would lead to a solid foundation for a partnership. It turned out that the man was thinking of launching an enterprise, either alone or with an associate. Based on my explanation, he chose the partnership, and did not regret the decision. The point is to let your intuition guide you. Sometimes you may interpret a symbol one way for one cup, and differently for another cup, depending on surrounding images and guidance from your inner voice.

I cannot emphasize enough that if you want to become a serious reader, you should keep a log of the cups you have read and the ways in which you interpreted the symbols. When you understand your proclivities and biases, you will more accurately and quickly produce interpretations.

5. Discover special signs. These are the unusual formations or images that mean something distinctive to either you or the inquirer. Once when reading for a young woman, I came across an image of a mouse. Generally, mice stand for small thefts, lost opportunities, arguments among friends and family, or a

timid personality. This particular mousie, however, looked very cute, with tiny glasses perched on its nose and a granny hat. I asked my client what this little rodent signified to her. A wide smile spread across her face, and she replied, "The mouse is my totem animal. I keep little mice figurines and talismans all over my home." For this client, the mouse signified domestic bliss, and I interpreted it in that way for her cup.

Occasionally you may spot a symbol you can't find in a dictionary. When this happens, use your intuition to come up with a meaning. For instance, if you see an image of a kitchen blender, it may mean that the inquirer is being advised to blend ideas from many different sources into a synergistic whole.

6. Determine the balance of positive and negative signs. Bigger figures carry more weight than smaller ones. Groups of images are often more significant than singletons, unless the lone image is quite large. Clear images are more important than muddy ones. Weak symbols may refer to a confused state of mind rather than events likely to occur. A cup full of clumps may indicate that the inquirer's life is brimming with trouble. When you view the cup from all angles, you may distinguish

two figures or even more in the same grouping. Every image you see is valid and interconnected. If symbols fall within a quarter-inch of each other, consider them mutually influential.

Timing Events

In my experience, the time span the leaves cover is generally not very long—perhaps three or four months. I believe that the leaves' propensity to be influenced is only strong enough to pick up clues from the recent past, present, or near future. Yet within this range, the information they reveal can be extremely accurate. For other readers, the time span may be longer. No one way of considering the leaves is more correct or better than another. Part of the beauty of tea leaf interpretation is that it is a personalized, malleable art, easily adapted to a variety of psyches— probably one reason for its widespread appeal.

There are several ways to map the time frame in which events are likely to take place, and no single approach is better than another. Choose the one with which you feel most comfortable. Although I have my favorite method, I occasionally select another one when it makes better sense for a particular cup.

In the first method, signs near the rim show occurrences that will take place sooner than those near the bottom. Events at the bottom of the cup will likely take place after three to four months. As the handle represents the inquirer, images that hover around it show the inquirer's immediate environment and activities. If, while you are reading, some leaves fall outside of the cup, it may indicate an event that already has occurred.

You can also take symbols that face the handle to mean events approaching the inquirer, while those facing away indicate departing influences. Some readers interpret the images to the left of the handle as signifying past events that are still influencing the present, while those to the right refer to occurrences yet to come.

In a third approach, the handle represents present time, and leaves grouped around it show what will occur within the next few days. Alternatively, the handle may indicate the inquirer's personality traits and mood, which may affect events. Moving clockwise around the cup, one-quarter of the way is one month, one-half is two months, and three-quarters, three months. The area to the right side of the handle shows four months. Events close to the rim will take place at the beginning of the month; those in the middle, toward the middle of the month; and those toward the bottom, but not directly on the bottom, will transpire at the end of a given month.

In this system, images at the bottom of the cup are valid throughout the entire four-month span.

Some readers prefer to locate events geographically in the cup. In this method, the handle represents south and highlights occurrences, people, or objects located south of the inquirer, or coming from that direction. Left of the handle represents west; right of the handle is east; and north is the position directly across from the handle.

Traditional tea leaf readers argue that what lies directly at the bottom of the cup and does not extend up the sides shows "troubles, tears, and tombstones." These interpreters also believe that the events found at the top of the cup will feel joyful and that the occurrences seen in the middle of the cup reflect the normal ebb and flow of daily life. In my experience, what remains at the bottom of the cup may not necessarily represent actual occurrences, but life's emotional, physical, and spiritual effects on the inquirer. Sometimes I interpret these images to represent what will remain in the background for the inquirer throughout the time period the reading covers.

Telling the Story

You are ready to weave your story. Tea leaf reading should be fun for both the inquirer and the interpreter. So tell an engaging tale based on the evidence.

If you interpret the symbols without a firm structure, your inquirer may be left with a fuzzy impression of the future. Build a strong narrative from the signs to lend coherence and continuity to your reading. Place together coupled events, and pay attention to the time-frame references and the effects on the inquirer shown at the bottom of the cup.

Once I read a cup where an airplane appeared to the left of the handle flying away over a mountain range. The mountains were coupled with several dots. Nearby, a chain pointed upward. Airplanes usually indicate air travel. Mountains stand for obstacles, but these peaks looked clear in the cup; that is, they were not obscured by other leaves. They were also coupled with several dots, which are positive signs. The image of a chain can mean a series of events, a commitment, or a constraint. The chain pointed upward in the cup, which was a good sign. This is how I interpreted the symbols for the inquirer:

"Within the next couple of weeks you will take a journey by air over the mountains. On this trip, one thing will lead to another. In the end, you will make quite a bit of money because you will have engaged in a profitable alliance with another individual or entity." Indeed, the inquirer was preparing to take a plane to California (over the Rockies from where we were) to discuss a possible business partnership with another firm.

As the above sample reading shows, some symbols reveal more than one meaning. A baby can stand for a new project; persistent, small worries; or an actual baby. An apron can refer to meeting and entertaining new friends, but can also show that the inquirer feels trapped in the home. A crab can single out a crabby acquaintance or enemy, or it may refer to a person born under the zodiac sign Cancer, or some important event that will occur in July. To pick the appropriate interpretation, pay attention to surrounding symbols and how everything fits into your narrative's flow.

Contradictory symbols sometimes arrange themselves in the cup. All I can suggest by way of explanation is that life is full of contradictions. This should come as no surprise to you or your inquirer. In these cases, make sure you give both sets of meanings so the inquirer can opt for the one that best fits the situation.

Some readers recommend that signs never be interpreted literally. Others prefer to convey a more literal meaning only if the symbol is linked to a number or a letter. For example, an image of a cat can show jealousy or a catty person. In my own cup, a figure of a cat sitting next to the letter *K* can only refer to my little white kitty, Klondike. I believe how you explain a sign depends on the other images in the cup and your own gut feeling. Look for nearby images to help you understand a symbol. A star by itself may mean success or inspiration. Coupled with a dancer, it may signify accomplishment in the arts. Linked to a book, the inquirer may soon study astronomy or a related field.

Your contemplating the cup should only last a few minutes, or your inquirer may grow impatient or anxious, fearing some looming catastrophe. With practice, you will be able to elicit the significant symbols in the cup quickly. Don't feel you need to find a meaning for every sign. Only interpret the ones that jump out at you.

Divination Ethics

Throughout the reading, stress the positive. If you say, "Gosh, I see the presentation you'll make to your company next month ending in a mess," your inquirer surely will be talked into botching it up. It's better to suggest, "As you prepare your presentation, make sure you conduct careful research, pay attention to details, and practice your delivery—the result will be a resounding success." As the excerpt from Dickens that I quoted at the beginning of chapter 2 implies, the inquirer is coming to you to find out what *may* happen, not what necessarily *will* happen. Everyone has the free will to change the probable course of events the reader lays out. This is why people have readings in the first place—your goal is to help inquirers gain clear perspectives on their lives.

It's also important to remain emotionally detached when giving a reading. If you absorb your inquirer's feelings—be they positive or negative—you will carry around the emotional charge for a long time. Build-up of emotional detritus from others can drag you down, drain your energy, and affect your emotions and even your physical well-being.

If you remain detached, you only transmit the information you see in the cup, not what the inquirer wants you to see. Occasionally after completing a reading, a client has told me I was full of hooey and stomped out only to call a month later and sheepishly verify that everything I interpreted happened. You simply can't let yourself get engaged, or you won't give your best effort. This is one reason some readers clear the air and ground themselves after giving a reading by blowing out candles, clapping their hands, or taking a break to find something to eat and drink.

Tips for Giving a Great Reading

- Relax yourself and your inquirers by engaging them in light chitchat while they are drinking. If the conversation doesn't flow naturally, or even if it does, regale them with fun facts about the history of tea or tea superstitions found in chapter 7.

- Go with your first impressions; they are usually correct.

- If, while contemplating the cup, an image pops into your mind's eye, do not hesitate to mention it, even if it is not replicated in the leaves.

- Weigh the number of positive symbols against negative ones (see chapter 8 for examples). Begin by telling your inquirer that it is a generally good cup, or one that shows challenges to overcome, or that the cup exhibits many love and romance symbols, money signs, or images relating to career.

- Answer your inquirer's stated questions first before moving on to other information.

- If you observe several negative symbols, let your inquirer know that he or she is there to perceive a *possible* outcome to a situation, not a result set in stone, and certainly not the only possible outcome. Tell your client these symbols represent cautions only. Armed with this information, the person has free will to change any negative scenarios that may surface.

- Do not hesitate to consult a symbols dictionary or the definitions listed in Part Two of this book to help you with your interpretations.

- If you get stuck on an interpretation, lay out the tarot cards or use another divinatory method, such as rune-casting or a pendulum, to help clarify images in the leaves.

- Keep in mind that images might carry a literal interpretation rather than a symbolic one. Sometimes a breadbox is just a breadbox!

- If your inquirers are ever unhappy with their readings, tell them that perhaps they have come with specific questions in mind. Subconsciously, another question has arisen that perhaps is more important, and that this question has now been answered. If inquirers still express doubt, you can always prepare a second cup to clarify the situation. If the questions still have not been answered satisfactorily and you have also used other forms of divination, the answers may not yet have solidified. At that point, it is best to put an end to the session and save further inquiries for a more propitious time.

Tea leaf reading is an entertaining and enriching experience for both inquirer and reader that will add to your depth of knowledge and enjoyment of tea. In the next chapter, I'll show you how to interpret the leaves, presenting four sample readings.

four

Sample Readings

Tea does our fancy aid,
Repress those vapours which the head invade,
And keeps that palace of the soul serene.

—EDMUND WALLER, "OF TEA"

You've already learned a lot about how to prepare and understand tea leaf symbols, but there's still one more hill to climb. Now, you're going to pull your facts together and spin an engaging yarn. When I started out, I selected and prepared tea like a tea master, got the cup ready to read in record time, and handily looked up symbol meanings. But when it came to interpreting the signs, my inquirers furrowed their brows and said things like, "Come again?" "I didn't quite understand what you said." "I don't know how what you say relates to my question."

That's when I decided I needed a personal trainer to help me reach the tea leaf reading summit.

By a personal trainer, I mean that I wanted to have examples under my belt of how to tell the tale before I felt confident scaling the mountain solo. In this book, there's only room for a few stories, but I hope they give you a good idea of how to proceed. As with any skill, practice makes perfect. The more cups you read, the better you'll become at interpreting them in a truthful but entertaining way.

In the four readings that follow, I sometimes choose a less common symbolic meaning because based on the inquirer's questions, my intuition came into play. Although I can't teach you how to use your intuition, I can open the door for you to allow yourself to use it. I also highlight the symbols found in the cups so you can more readily refer to them. Two photos that clearly delineate the images from both sides of each cup accompany the readings.

Cup 1: Republic of Tea Rose Petal Tea

For a Young Woman Who Yearns to Find True Love

This inquirer was especially interested in meeting her soul mate. For this reason, I chose a black tea scented with rose petals touted as the tea for "the Queen of Hearts." This blend, concocted by The Republic of Tea, has an outstanding flavor. It is such a favorite

Cup 1

with clients that I offer it when I do readings for large gatherings like weddings and fundraisers.

Right away in the home position under the handle, I spotted a **table** topped by **roses,** and in the bottom of the cup, a **flowery arch** appears. Before searching for other images, I told my inquirer that it seemed her wish would be granted soon, but that the cup has much more to tell. During the cup contemplation phase, I found the following key images:

Table with flowers (near the handle)—a festive gathering

Swan—desire fulfilled; a lover suddenly enters the picture

The letter *P*—joy, or someone whose name starts with "P"

Tulip—passion, something to do with the Netherlands

Fan coupled with two short sticks—advice against verbal indiscretion or flirtation, lunar powers, two women

Floral bouquet—happiness, romance, fulfillment

Flowery arch (at the bottom)—wishes fulfilled, trip to a faraway destination, roads open

After putting together my story in my mind, I began:

"When we put ourselves in the right frame of mind to attract our desires—money, friends, love, or whatever—we set up conditions that allow these desires to manifest. You have been preparing yourself mentally and emotionally to meet the right life partner because I see fulfillment in the bottom of the cup in the form of a **flowery archway**. The timing is right for you to achieve this aim.

"You will meet your gentleman very soon at a lively social gathering, as shown by the **flower-topped table** and the **swan**. His name may begin with the letter **P**. You will fall passionately in love, and perhaps even take a trip to Holland together, as this pretty **tulip** indicates.

"On your return, you may stir up jealousy from two women—do you see the **two short sticks**? They may try to force your relationship to break off by spreading false rumors about you to your lover, and they may even flirt with him. During this time, I advise you to be quite discreet with everything you say and do as to your relationship, for you don't want to give these ladies ammunition. The picture of the **fan** tells me these things.

"Once you make it over that hump, joy and happiness is yours. Although I cannot predict wedding bells within the next four months, I do see a lovely **floral bouquet**, which shows that the relationship is solid and loving, and that the road opens for you and your lover to either travel or live in a faraway destination for a while."

Cup 2: Chamomile from My Garden
For a Man with Health Issues

The following reading was performed for a man with declining health. At the time, he was waiting for test results from his doctor. His demeanor was anxious and his wish was for a clean bill of health.

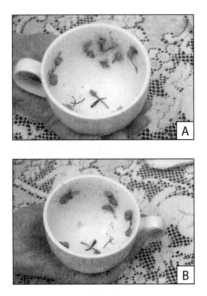

Cup 2

A quick glance at his cup told me he had reason to be worried. I didn't want to alarm him, so before I did a thorough examination of the cup, I told him:

"Your cup does reveal your concern over health matters. Indeed, something seems to be going on in this area, but these two enormous **crosses** in the bottom of the cup point to protection and a long life. Let me study your cup for a few moments to see if I can shed more light on the topic."

Meanings for the significant images followed:

Two crosses—a long life, protection, feeling troubled

Bones—health advisory, environmental toxins

Clock in middle of cup—serious illness, but the patient will recover

Female profile wearing nurse's cap—help from a health professional

Bee—domestic bliss, good news

Perched bird—waiting for news

After organizing my thoughts, I began:

"The **crossed bones** near the handle of your cup shows that you have a health issue that may possibly stem from environmental toxins. The **clock** in the middle of the cup indicates that the illness is serious, but you will recover. In fact, you will receive help from a female health professional who may be a nurse, judging from the **nurse's cap** on her head. This woman will help with your recovery.

"As presaged by the little **bee** flying toward you and the **perched bird**, in a couple of months, you will receive good news about your illness. In fact, the signs are so positive that I believe you will make a full recovery. As I mentioned before, the **two crosses** at the bottom of the cup indicate that yours will be a very long life."

Note: I mentioned many more images to the inquirer than I have mentioned here. I chose to highlight only those symbols that related directly to his problem because of his troubled state. I didn't mention the other symbols here either because many were too light to photograph. Chamomile tea often behaves this way: the flowers cling together to make a few bold pictures, and the residue creates light background images.

Cup 3—San Francisco Herb Company Gunpowder Green

For a Man Who Needs to Make a Business Decision

Recently, a man came to me in a quandary over a business issue. Another man had approached him about going into business together to buy a chicken farm, and he even offered to put up a large sum to help with the purchase. My inquirer entered into the partnership even though he didn't know the other man very well. Now his intuition was telling him that he would regret the alliance. So he wanted to know what the tea leaves had to say—which was plenty!

A quick glance revealed an **open umbrella** at the bottom of the cup, so I told my inquirer that no matter what, he would be protected from complete failure. These are the significant symbols I distinguished:

> **Open umbrella**—protection, troubles will pass
>
> **Square**—a tight spot
>
> **Face with feather in hat**—an insincere, unpredictable person

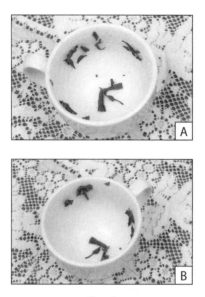

Cup 3

Scissors—severing a relationship

Acorn—a good investment

Tree—a wish fulfilled

Fat airplane—big return flying toward the inquirer

I began my reading with, "Well, it looks like your intuition is on target. Do you see the **square** coupled with the **profile of a man's face with a feather on his head**? It seems as if your partner is unpredictable, unreliable and may not be telling you everything about his financial situation. Perhaps he has bad debts or is trying to misrepresent the chicken farm to you in some way. The square shows that very shortly this man will back you into a tight spot. You will need to sever the relationship completely, as the **scissors** indicate, and abandon the chicken farm. You will incur a monetary loss but be a wiser person for it.

"Good news is on the way. A couple of months after you have recovered from this fiasco, an opportunity will present itself to you to make another investment. You will do this investment on your own, and it is a judicious one. At least, this is what the **little acorn** tells me. From the acorn, a **large oak tree** will grow, so for the small amount you invest, you will yield a big return, as shown by the **fat airplane** loaded with bounty, flying toward the tree."

Cup 4: Twinings Earl Grey

For a Woman Who Wants
Something Better out of Life

This woman came to me for a general reading. While she drank her tea, she expressed dissatisfaction with her job and life. As I began to examine her cup, to the right of the handle I immediately noticed a humped line reminding me of **hills**. At the bottom I spotted a **candle** with sparks emitting from the flame. To allay her immediate concerns before settling down to see what else her future held, I told her that although obstacles blocked her path at the moment, something quite wonderful would happen soon to change her perspective on life. Then I fell silent for a few minutes while contemplating the rest of her cup. I distinguished these major images:

Hills (near the handle)—obstacles

Ant (at bottom of the first hill)—hard work

Bouncing ball (nearby)—bouncing back from adversity, restlessness

Cactus (farther along)—Arizona, courage

Pyramid—long-abiding spirituality

Profile of man's head speaking *and*

Candle with sparks made from three short sticks—enlightenment, meeting three people, probably women

It was then time to put my story together. I began: "This cup clearly reveals the trouble you are having at work. You feel like an **ant** patiently climbing and descending **hills**, but at the end of the day, you are left with no real feeling of accomplishment. You grow restless (the **bouncing ball**) and yearn to get away."

Here I paused and asked a question, the answer to which would determine the direction of the rest of the reading, as I wasn't sure whether to treat the

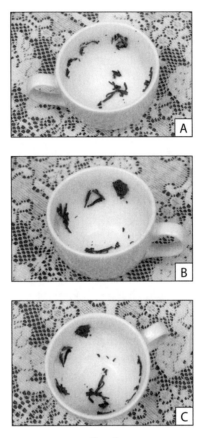

Cup 4

cactus as representing courage or whether its meaning was more literal. The plant may even symbolize both ideas. "Are you contemplating taking a vacation to the Southwest?"

Startled, my inquirer replied, "I just got a flyer in my inbox advertising a spiritual retreat for managers and executives in Arizona. It looks intriguing."

I nodded. "If you go on this retreat—and I believe this will happen—you will discover a way to regenerate body, mind, and spirit. The **profile of the man's head**, who, judging from the dot flowing out of his mouth, is speaking, tells me that you may listen to some enlightening lectures given by a man. You may also make friends with **three women** as shown by these **three sparks** emanating from the candle at the bottom of the cup. They will guide you along a path toward spiritual wisdom, symbolized by the **pyramid**. The **candle** at the bottom of the cup shows that you have desired enlightenment and regeneration for a long time, and you have put yourself in the position to accept the gifts flowing from Spirit.

————

Now that you know how to relate your teacup story and probably have taken your first flights with newly sprouted tea leaf reader wings, it's time to revisit the subject of herbs. Some people who do not tolerate caffeine well or have religious or health reasons to not drink tea may still want a reading. Next, we'll delve more deeply into the realm of herbal infusions.

five

Herbal Infusions and Decoctions

Herbal tea brings pleasant dreams;
Beauty, health and wealth, it seems.

—Mitzie Stuart Keller,
Mysterious Herbs and Roots

Not long ago, I toured the Celestial Seasonings home office and factory in Boulder, Colorado. In one room, fragrant, forty-pound sacks of black tea stood stacked to the ceiling waiting to be blended. Guest Relations Manager Steve Spencer escorted me into the peppermint room. Bags brimming with peppermint leaves exuded such a heady menthol fragrance that, it was explained to me, the room needed to be sealed off so the strong aroma wouldn't filter into other teas. Mr. Spencer told me that when he shows visitors this room, he usually pauses to explain the difference between tea and herbal infusions. He finds that many assume the company's herbal infusions are made from decaffeinated combinations of black or green teas.

Only a beverage made from the *Camellia sinensis* plant can truly be called a tea. Technically speaking, drinks concocted from other botanicals are herbal infusions, tisanes, or herbal decoctions. Because the general public calls these brews "teas," some retail tea companies, including the famous Celestial Seasonings and The Republic of Tea, also refer to their botanical blends as herbal teas.

Herbal infusions are addressed in this chapter partly because they taste good and are good for you. For these reasons, many of my tea leaf reading clients request that I prepare herbal drinks instead of tea. Equally important for teacup reading, botanicals have acquired so many symbolic meanings in folklore that they make ideal choices for theme readings. A vital reason for learning more about herbal beverages is to know which ones may be harmful so they aren't used by mistake.

What Herbal Infusions Can Do for You

Herbal beverages have been brewed since primitive times, both as flavorful refreshments and as remedies. Chinese medicine is based, in part, on prescribing strongly brewed herbal drinks called decoctions. Botanicals tend to act more subtly and gently on the system than pharmaceuticals. Besides attacking the symptoms of specific maladies, they address the entire body holistically. When you swallow a capsule, it goes directly to your stomach and never touches your taste buds. When you drink an herbal infusion, beginning in the mouth, the liquid follows a steady path through your digestive system, which makes for more efficient absorption. Herbal blends are relatively cheap, too. Most boxes of twenty to twenty-four herbal teabags cost less than six dollars.

Many botanicals also provide small amounts of essential vitamins and minerals. They can stimulate or suppress the appetite, settle the stomach, control the bowels, ease cold and flu symptoms, cleanse and purify the blood, act as a tonic, stimulate or relax the body, and alleviate an assortment of symptoms from high blood pressure to venereal disease. Nonetheless, you should never assume that botanical infusions substitute for a healthy diet and lifestyle—they are meant to be drunk as supplements only.

Taking Precautions

I cannot overstress that you do research before attempting to alleviate symptoms of illness or disease by drinking herbal beverages. While the effects of many botanicals are mild, others can be highly narcotic, intoxicating, or deadly, even in small amounts. For instance, an infusion concocted from a poisonous plant like water hemlock or black hellebore can kill you. After all, this is how Socrates met his demise. In a more recent sad case, a Colorado teen bought a pound of poppy seeds—not the illegal opium poppy, but rather the kind we all use for baked goods. Trouble was, he brewed a strong decoction from the seeds and drank a large quantity of it to get high. The boy fell into a coma and died. World-class athletes know not to even eat one poppy seed roll before undergoing drug testing, or they will test positive for barbiturates.

Always tell your physician about any botanicals you plan to take. This way, you will receive a professional opinion about their safety and find out which might interfere with prescribed pharmaceuticals. Children and pregnant women should only drink specific herbal infusions with their doctors' consent, as many otherwise safe substances could have adverse effects on their delicate constitutions.

To broaden your knowledge of botanicals beyond this book, I suggest you read other works exclusively dedicated to herbal infusions and decoctions. You can supplement your knowledge by researching on the Internet, or by asking a knowledgeable salesperson at an herbal supply or natural foods store.

Tea Botanicals to Avoid during Pregnancy

If a mother-to-be comes to you for a reading, you should know which herbs to avoid. While many botanicals fit this category, only a handful of them are regularly used for beverage-making. Given the parameters of this book, I only list common potentially harmful ones. For a complete list, check out pregnancy websites such as www.motherlove.com and www.naturalark.com, both wonderful sites with a wealth of information. Everybody's physical constitution is different, so what one pregnant woman may tolerate well, another will not abide. I remember when I was pregnant, the sight and smell of black tea—usually my favorite—nauseated me. Thank goodness that condition didn't last, or I would never have written this book!

The following botanicals make the list because they affect the hormones, are too strong or irritating, or can bring on bleeding or contractions. They include: aloe vera, angelica, barberry, bee balm, black cohosh, blue cohosh, black walnut, blessed thistle, borage, buckthorn, cascara sagrada, catnip, chaste tree berry, chicory, damiana, dong quai, elecampane, fenugreek, feverfew, gentian, goldenseal, horehound, licorice, lovage, motherwort, Oregon grape root, osha, parsley, rosemary, sage, sarsaparilla, Siberian ginseng, thyme, turmeric, and yarrow. See the Common Poisonous Plants section on page 88 for more.

How to Prepare
Herbal Infusions and Decoctions

If you hanker to boil up your own botanical brews, here's how to go about it. First, be aware that you prepare a medicinal potion somewhat differently from an herbal beverage or a *Camellia sinensis* tea. I already discussed brewing beverage teas in chapter 2 and will offer more details about herbal beverage infusions shortly. To make a medicinal infusion, add two or three fresh sprigs or two dried teaspoonfuls of flowers and leaves to 1½ cups cold, filtered water. Boil for ten minutes, and simmer for five more minutes until the liquid is reduced by one-third.

Boil and simmer for twice the time (twenty minutes and ten minutes respectively), and you get a medicinal decoction. These strong-tasting liquids are commonly made from roots and seeds, so it takes a longer brewing time to release their essence.

Picking Your Own

A splendid way to obtain fresh, healthy, lip-smacking herbs is to pick your own. If you don't grow an herb garden or you choose to gather your botanicals in the wild, take care not to harvest ones that have been doused with pesticides. Never take plants from the roadside because they are the ones most exposed to pesticides, car emissions, and other pollutants.

Most herbal beverage drinks are made from leaves such as peppermint and sage, and from flowers like chamomile and rose. Occasionally you will also use seeds like fennel and dill, and barks like sassafras and cinnamon. If you harvest flowers and leaves, the best season to gather seeds and fruit is when they ripen. Pick flowers and leaves in early to midsummer when the essential oils are most concentrated. Folk wisdom dictates that around St. John's Day (June 24) is the best time. Harvest before ten AM, when essential oils and nutrients are flowing strongest. Never pick more than one-third of the plant to give it a good chance to regenerate. And don't forget to take along a plant identification book with pictures to help you avoid picking poisonous plants.

Back home, rinse your harvest thoroughly in cold water to remove dust and clinging dirt. Use the botanicals fresh, or tie them in bunches and hang upside down from the ceiling in a cool, dry, dark place with good air circulation. Your basement, airing closet, gardening shed, or barn work fine. Tie together only small amounts of botanicals. As this voice of experience can relate, big bunches tend to grow mold because the air does not circulate freely around them. It is truly disconcerting to have to consign all those lovingly harvested but now useless bunches of herbs to the compost heap. I also suggest you label your bunches since dried herbs tend to look alike. I use the tie-on labels for pricing clothing at garage sales. After the botanicals have thoroughly dried, remove leaves and flowers from the stems and crush the leaves. Keep flowers whole and dice stems and roots if you want to use them, too.

Place each plant part in a separate airtight container. For example, don't put dandelion leaves and dandelion roots in the same jar, as each part of this plant has a distinctive flavor and is used for a different reason. Store your containers in a cool place away from the light.

Herbal Medicine Chest:
Ten Botanicals to Keep in Stock

The following represent typical botanicals that make first-rate medicinal infusions and decoctions because of their action on the body. Not coincidentally, they taste good for tea leaf reading, too. Unless otherwise indicated, prepare the leaves and flowers in an infusion.

Alfalfa *(Medicago sativa)*

This grassy perennial is a ready source of minerals such as potassium, magnesium, phosphorus, and calcium; vitamins A, B, C, and K; organic salts; and essential enzymes. Alfalfa's attributes include its use as a nutritive tonic and weight loss facilitator. The herb helps decrease fevers, cure infections, arrest hemorrhage, lower blood pressure, and hasten recovery from illness. The light-colored grass renders designs similar to those formed by white tea in tea leaf reading.

Althea Root, also known as Marshmallow Plant (Althaea officinalis)
The mucilage derived from the root soothes skin and mucous membranes. A decoction placates sore throats and internal and external inflammations.

Angelica (Angelica archangelica)
This plant's many virtues include its use as a diuretic, expectorant, digestive stimulant, and tonic for circulation and for when the body needs an extra push. A decoction of the seeds banishes flatulence. The decoction concocted from the root combats nausea and helps cure colds, colic, pleurisy, coughs, and urinary tract infections.

Chamomile (Matricaria recutita)
The apple-scented, daisy-like flower of this bright, sturdy little herb is the part used to make infusions. Drink it to get a good night's sleep. Chamomile is also a digestive, and helps lactating mothers increase milk production. It is one of the most popular selections for tea leaf reading.

Dandelion (Taraxacum officinale)

Both the leaves and root of this cheery, yellow-flowered plant ubiquitous in the springtime garden are used. Dandelion stimulates excretion of urine to help cure urinary and kidney infections, and is effective in dissolving kidney stones. The high vitamin C content benefits cases of eczema and scurvy. Besides making a superior-tasting brew, you can eat dandelion leaves fresh in a salad. Roasted dandelion root is a coffee substitute, and can make a reasonable tea leaf reading choice for the coffee drinker. Because most dandelions you are likely to run across grow in lawns and parks, make sure they haven't been sprayed with pesticides or chemical fertilizers before you pick them.

Ginger (Zingiber officinale)

The silvery-brown root stalk of this aromatic, tropical perennial is more than a zesty culinary spice. Drink the stimulating tea to overcome motion or morning sickness, diarrhea, and flatulent colic, and to alleviate chest complaints. Ginger stimulates the digestion to help with weight loss. Besides its many virtues as a beverage, ginger makes a piquant addition to pumpkin pie and many other desserts and sauces. In tea leaf reading, the stalks have a propensity toward forming numbers and letters.

Lemon Balm *(Melissa officinalis)*

This refreshing, lemony-tasting beverage, perfect for summertime tea leaf reading, is brewed from the leaves. Lemon balm helps reduce fevers and acts as a sedative, gentle stimulant, and tonic. Lemon balm also regulates menstrual flow and soothes sore throats, aching teeth, and the pain from bee stings.

Nettles *(Urtica dioica)*

Also know as stinging nettle because the fresh leaves are incredibly irritating to skin until they are dried, this versatile plant nevertheless is valuable in herbal medicine. It is a blood purifier, expectorant, and astringent that also mitigates asthma symptoms, regulates the female reproductive system, and aids weight loss. Because nettles are rich in iron, they counteract anemia. The dried leaves make lacy designs in tea leaf reading. This botanical also increases mineral assimilation. If you get tired of drinking it, pour it on your hair as a rinse to stimulate hair growth.

Peppermint *(Mentha piperita)*

The leaves of this hardy perennial plant of the mint family—famous as an ingredient in gum, candy, and lozenges—make a delicious edible garnish. Peppermint also serves as an antispasmodic, disinfectant, and nerve tonic. It relieves symptoms of colds and the flu, headache, nausea, rheumatism, sore throat, and toothache. My tea leaf reading clients who pass on black tea often choose peppermint as an alternative. The leaves make lacy designs on the inside of the that cup I find fun to interpret.

Raspberry *(Rubus idaeus)*

This prickly bush that grows near water is famous for its sweet red or black berries. The tasty leaf is valuable in infusions as an antispasmodic, astringent, and stimulant. Raspberry is regarded as one of the best remedies to relieve menstrual cramps and strengthen the uterus during pregnancy. The leaves are also good for stomach upsets, fevers, colds, flu, canker sores— and of course, for tea leaf reading.

Common Poisonous Plants to Avoid

In addition to those listed on page 81, here are more plants you should never ingest: bloodroot, calamus, camphor, castor bean, Christmas rose, comfrey, datura, deer's tongue, iris, lily of the valley, lobelia, mistletoe, mugwort, pennyroyal, periwinkle, southernwood, sweet woodruff, tansy, thuja, water hemlock, and wormwood.

Designer Infusions

Now that you've been introduced to herbal infusions, you might want to test your creativity as a blender by preparing what I call a "designer infusion." Simply put, designer infusions are herbal blends that you create especially for your personal needs, tastes, and special tea leaf readings. Following is a list of twenty common complaints, with four botanicals for each one from which you can assemble your own "prescription."

To discover which flavors you like best and how the substances interact with your body, I suggest you first try them as "singles," then as "doubles," "triples," and finally, as "quadruples." That is to say, test them one at a time as a drink. Then try combining two, experimenting with the ratios until you find what best suits you. Do the same with three botanicals, and finally combine all four.

For example, to make a Stress-Be-Gone infusion, you might buy some dried lemon balm leaves, hops flowers, feverfew flowers, and licorice powder at your local grocer or herbalist supply store. Make separate infusions from one teaspoon of each botanical. Next, mix together ½ teaspoon lemon balm and ½ teaspoon hops, and decide how you like this tisane. Another time, blend an infusion from ½ teaspoon lemon balm, ¼ teaspoon feverfew, and ¼ teaspoon hops.

Your final recipe might consist of ½ teaspoon lemon balm, ¼ teaspoon feverfew, ⅛ teaspoon hops, and a dash or two of licorice powder. Or, you may prefer lemon balm exclusively, with a dash of licorice powder to awaken the lemony taste. Then again, perhaps you'll be bowled over by one of the other single herbs—you musn't be afraid to experiment.

Twenty Common Maladies and Botanicals to Alleviate Them

The following herbs have been used for centuries in folk medicine to relieve common ailments. If an inquirer comes to you complaining about one of these, you can whip up a personalized herbal blend and say you're offering a double bang for their buck.

Arthritis—devil's claw root, marjoram, nettles, tarragon

Bladder infection—cranberry, couch grass, dandelion, parsley

Colds—birch leaf, ginger root, lemon balm, licorice root

Constipation—dill weed, ginger root, lemon peel, strawberry leaves

Cough—elecampane, red clover, coltsfoot, horehound

Diarrhea—bistort, cinquefoil, life everlasting, Solomon's seal

Fatigue—elder flowers, ginseng, rosemary, sage

Fever—blessed thistle, borage, feverfew, lovage

Headache—lady's slipper, lavender, peppermint, rosemary. (Since lady's slipper is becoming rare, to "go green" you might substitute kola nut. Be aware that the result will be a completely different flavor, both separately and in combination.)

Hemorrhage—alfalfa, goldenseal, nettles, saffron

Indigestion/Gas—angelica, fennel, passionflower, peppermint

Inflammation—caraway, chamomile, chicory, coltsfoot

Insomnia—catnip (I especially like the lemon-flavored variety), hops, chamomile, valerian root

Liver tonic—dandelion, hops, milk thistle, nettles

Nausea—angelica, galangal, ginger root, rosemary

Sore throat—althea root, bladderwrack, borage, lavender

Stress—hops, lemon balm, licorice, skullcap

Tonic—Irish moss, lady's mantle, parsley root, wood betony

Toothache—clove, lavender, lemon balm,
peppermint

Weight loss—alfalfa, bladderwrack, fennel,
guaraná

Herbal Recipes

Following are two of my own favorite herbal blend
recipes.

Slim Jane Tea

This recipe is for anyone fasting for any reason,
though especially to lose weight. I find it convenient
to make a lot of this tea at one time, but add only
one teaspoonful per cup of hot water. Combine ¼
cup blackberry leaves, ¼ cup alfalfa, ¼ cup nettles,
1 teaspoon buchu, 1 teaspoon psilium husks, 1 teaspoon sage, 1 teaspoon crushed rosehips, ¼ teaspoon
crushed juniper berries, and ¼ teaspoon licorice root
powder.

Lucky Day Prosperity Tea

Chamomile and peppermint are alleged to confer
wealth and prosperity. Both botanicals are readily
available at grocery stores and are easy to grow, if
you are so inclined. Add ½ teaspoonful of chamomile flowers and ½ teaspoonful of the peppermint
leaves to a cup of boiling water. Steep for three minutes and enjoy a delicious drink. Easy as pie!

Tasty Herbal Brews

Don't feel compelled to drink herbal beverages just because they are good for you. Many tisanes are flavorful enough to be consumed for pleasure. You can brew up a hot drink anytime from virtually any single or combination of two or three edible botanicals whose flavors you like. To clue yourself in on compatible flavors and extend your range, get to be a "label hound" and study ingredients' labels of your favorite herbal blends at the grocery or health food stores.

Common pleasant-tasting beverage herbs that are also suitable for tea leaf reading include: angelica root, bergamot mint, chamomile, chicory, coltsfoot, fennel seed, dandelion (leaves or root), eyebright, lavender, lemon balm, rose petals, nettles, peppermint, red clover blossoms, raspberry, sage, sarsaparilla root, spearmint, and violet. Use the leaves and flowers only unless otherwise specified. Remember you can also flavor black, green, and oolong teas with herbs and flowers.

Brew a beverage tea as you would black tea. Use half the amount of dried herbs as you would for a medicinal infusion (see the directions on page 82). If you're lucky enough to find a source of fresh herbs, put twice as many in the pot as you would dried, as fresh flavors are not as concentrated. Bottoms up!

————

Whether you're drinking black, white, oolong, or green tea or herbal infusions, I hope you're excited to start tea leaf reading, because now it's your turn to tread the boards and tip those cups. With your script in hand and all those rehearsals behind you, I'm confident you'll be a successful reader. The next chapter will help you set a stage for your performances.

six

Tantalizing Tea Parties

Never trust a man who, when left alone in a
room with a tea cozy, doesn't try it on.

— BILLY CONNOLLY,
MUSICIAN AND COMEDIAN

You're loaded with more information about tea than a camel in a Russian tea caravan and, presumably, have practiced reading on yourself, close relatives, and friends. "Now," you inquire, "how do I bring my cupful of knowledge and expertise to a wider audience?" I thought you'd never ask.

The simple and straightforward answer is, host a tea party. Tea parties are logical and convenient venues to hone your tea leaf reading skills. In this chapter, you'll refine your skills in orchestrating a symphony of tea events for everyone's enjoyment.

Theme Tea Parties

In the first place, festivities don't need to revolve around teacup reading exclusively. You can slip in the divination as part of the light entertainment while everyone is chattering away and nibbling on finger food. Tea party themes are as limitless as your imagination. Simply make or buy invitations, place cards, and decorations to express your unique theme. Choose teas and foods that reflect the mood, and you're well on your way to creating an unforgettable afternoon or evening of fun and relaxation for you and your guests.

Consider these themes: Baby Shower Tea, Birthday Tea, Bridal Shower Tea, Chase Away Winter Blues Tea, Color Tea (where everything is the same color, including food, decorations, and dress), Children's Mad Hatter Tea, Tinkerbell Tea (or Wee Tee, as they are sometimes called), Autumn Tea, Garden Party Tea, Halloween Tea, Historical Tea, Boston Tea Party, Housewarming Tea, Mother/Daughter Tea, Mother/Son Tea, Red Hat Society Tea, Romance Tea, Shapes Tea (where everything is made into the same shape, including napkins, food, and decorations), Tea for Two, Wedding Tea, and—the very best kind of tea party—the No Special Reason At All Tea.

Highs and Lows of Taking Tea

When I started investigating tea parties, I bumped up against a wall of insurmountable vocabulary that confounded me. For example, do you know the difference between Afternoon Tea and High Tea, and assuming that some teas are called High Teas, whether Low Teas also exist? If you can answer those questions, you're doing better than I was, and you can skip to the next section. If you can't, please read on.

Afternoon Tea refers to the meal served up in most tearooms and many hotels traditionally between the hours of three and five o'clock, although nowadays, you often can find it offered from late morning into early evening. This meal was invented by Anna, the Countess of Bedford in the mid-1800s. This sensible, titled lady decided she could do with a cuppa and light repast to tide her over between lunch and a late dinner. She invited a few friends to her table, and "Afternoon Tea" was born. The style in which this meal is served can be formal or informal—a matter we'll discuss soon.

Besides taking the edge off your appetite, the idea behind Afternoon Tea is to relax and converse. Both reasons contribute to the custom of supplying the food in Lilliputian-size pieces. Afternoon Tea is also known as **Low Tea** because it is served at a low coffee table or side table, not at the dining table.

Subsets, so to speak, of Afternoon Tea include **Light Tea**, where tea, scones, and sweets are served. A fashionable kind of tea is a **Cream Tea**, where in addition to the tea and scones, jam, and Devonshire cream are added. A **Full Tea**, the kind most people are familiar with, supplies tea, savories, scones, sweets, and dessert.

In contrast, **High Tea** is served at the higher dining room table, but this is not its only distinguishing feature. High Tea was invented in England during the nineteenth century. As the price of tea became more affordable to the working class, laborers returning home half-starved after a hard day's work demanded their evening meal right away—as early as five or six o'clock. Wives obliged by rustling up a hearty meal eaten at the dining table, which included meat and kidney pies, baked beans, cheese, potatoes, bread, butter, and other filling food, all washed down with strong black tea. Because of the substantial fare, this meal is also called a **Meat Tea**.

Formal or Informal?

Given its purpose to satisfy the hunger of those who have spent a long day at physical labor, High Tea is usually an informal family affair. On the other hand, Afternoon Tea can be formal or informal. Formal teas are served on the best china over white linen tablecloths with matching linen napkins. Guests are expected to dress up. When taking tea at the Ritz in London, for example, women are asked to wear a long skirt or at least a semiformal dress. For men, a tie and coat are requirements. The Ritz is popular enough, especially with tourists, that you usually need to book at least a week ahead. By the way, if you are ever privileged enough to be invited to take tea with the Queen of England, protocol dictates that you may only eat what the Queen eats. If she ate a big lunch or—heaven forbid—is on a diet and chooses to nibble on only a crust of brown bread at a table groaning with goodies, you must follow suit.

Very Special Teas

If you feel like pulling out all the stops, you can host some elaborate teas. **The Japanese Tea Ceremony** represents the ultimate formal tea party. A model of elegance and grace, participants are knowledgeable about a wide array of disciplines. These include learning to prepare and serve the special powdered green tea called *matcha* in little round bowls, arrange flowers, and prepare the setting. One is bound to follow a rigid set of comportment rules that must not be broken. The Chinese **Gongfu** style of preparing and serving tea, though also complex, takes place in a more casual environment.

If either tradition sounds interesting to you, I suggest reading up before getting involved. I include some of my favorite works and websites that describe these ceremonies in the bibliography. With the growing interest in Asian cultures, societies of tea lovers adept at practicing this art have proliferated around the country. Use Google to find groups in your area to see if you can participate in these intricate but satisfying rituals.

If you prefer something less highly structured, but different from the everyday cup of tea, you might want to take a tip from my Russian ancestors. They often served India, China, Russian Caravan, or fruity herbal infusions from a samovar poured hot into a glass with a slice of lemon. In the summertime, you may want to fill the samovar with Moroccan mint tea. This Gunpowder Green tea flavored with mint and sweetened with lots of sugar or honey is poured with ceremony from a long-spouted pot into beautiful glasses. If you're feeling adventurous, you can host a yerba maté party. Yerba maté is grown in Argentina, and the people of the pampas have developed a ritual for drinking this herbal infusion that includes a gourd and a silver straw called a *bombilla*. (See my blog for more information. The URL is at the back of this book.) The joy of tea parties is that you can make them as formal as you want, or you can hold them in a laid-back setting at a picnic table in a park or with family in the living room to read everyone's leaves.

Tea Manners: It's All about R-E-S-P-E-C-T

Aretha Franklin sang it right. No matter what kind of soirée you hold, remember that the theory behind hosting a tea is to treat others in a social environment with respect, kindness, consideration, and politeness.

This philosophy is so rooted in the art of tea that the tea party has actually helped criminals "turn over a new leaf," as it were. Offenders from the Santa Fe, New Mexico, municipal court system can choose to be sentenced to taking tea. Now that's what I call hard labor! Seriously, Judge Frances Gallegos came up with this unique way to help offenders de-stress, control their emotions, and esteem others. Inmates enroll in a program where they engage in the Japanese tea ceremony, along with tai chi classes, meditation, and acupuncture. Students report that this combination of practices encourages them to stop abusing alcohol and drugs. They claim they are able to relax enough to reflect on their past actions, achieve a sense of inner balance, and feel a profound sense of well-being. Now isn't that just the prescription many of us living in the contemporary world outside prison are seeking? And it's a great excuse— as if one is needed—to throw a tea party.

Tea Leaf Reading Party

By now, you've probably settled on your theme and are raring to have a go at helping others achieve a sense of well-being in a welcoming environment and find out about their futures in the bargain. Following is an example of what I do to host a tea leaf reading party.

Preparations

Two weeks before the party, I send invitations to five of my closest friends. An invitation in the mail is a polite way to show I respect my guests. In the invitation decorated with enlarged images of tea leaves I pull from the Internet, I tell my friends we are going to read leaves. That way, they know what to expect and can come with questions ready. To foster an atmosphere of times gone by, I ask women to wear a long dress and old-fashioned hat, if they have one. My male guests are requested to wear slacks and sports jackets, but no ties, because that might make them uncomfortable.

I design place cards for each guest from heavy cardstock and write in calligraphy famous names from tea history so that guests, if they wish, can take on the role of one of these celebrities of the tea world.

As for the tea, I create simple favors, which consist of scoops of a loose tea—a favorite of mine is

Darjeeling scented with rose petals and lavender—poured into tiny resealable plastic bags. I place the little bags in the center of three-inch muslin squares. Then I gather up the ends of the squares and tie them with colored ribbon. Between the ribbon and muslin I insert a miniature aluminum scoop spoon, readily available at culinary supply stores, natural food grocers, or herb shops. Guests can take home their favors and scoop the tea from the muslin sachets to prepare individual cups.

On the day before the event, I set my table. For this particular example, I use Noritake Gold Queen china, Queen Elizabeth Coronation silver, Waterford crystal, and Royal Doulton candlesticks. Even though I cover the table with a Smithsonian angel lace tablecloth, I use paper napkins instead of lace or linen ones for a tea leaf reading party. Why? My guests and I are going to wreak havoc on the napkins when we empty the last teaspoonfuls of liquid on them to read our leaves.

The candles are handmade, of green tea-scented, pink beeswax I sell in my mail-order business. I understand most of my readers do not have such supplies at their fingertips. You can purchase unscented beeswax candles in many shops, and find green tea fragrance on Internet retail perfume sites to anoint your candles. As a final preparation, even though I intend to hold the tea at four o'clock in the afternoon, I close the drapes to create a romantic setting enhanced by the magic of candlelight.

I place tongs beside the three-tiered serving plate for guests to take their goodies, and include a plate of thinly sliced lemon and dishes of jam, cream, and lemon curd. If this were not a tea leaf reading party where we need to keep our cups relatively unadulterated, I would add a bowl of sugar cubes that dissolve quickly in the hot tea as well as milk. Never use cream, because it does not combine well with tea—it curdles and leaves an unappetizing scum.

Napkin Etiquette

Once you and your guests are seated at the table, open your napkin and place it on your lap. If you are wearing lipstick, be sure to blot it before you take your first sip so you don't leave an unsightly stain on the cup. When not using your napkin, keep it on your lap. Until the party is over, the napkin should never touch the table. Leave it on your chair if you need to get up for a few minutes. The host or hostess will signal the tea is over by placing the napkin loosely to the left of the plate. You should do the same as you rise to leave.

Setting the Mood

On the day before the event, I prepare the sandwich fillings and make certain I have all the ingredients together to bake the rest of the food. I choose my teas and get out the pots. On the morning of the tea, I bake the cake and scones, slice the cake into squares, and store the baked goods under plastic wrap. An hour before my guests arrive, I build the sandwiches. To ensure the tea is piping hot and delicious, I prepare it as my guests are arriving.

During the tea, I play soft classical or Celtic background music. Once we settle in to read our cups, and if my guests don't already know what to do, I give a short extemporaneous talk on reading the leaves. Each person makes a wish, and we read our own cups. Then we pour fresh cups and everyone makes another wish before drinking. When we finish the second cup, we give our cups to our neighbor to the left for an outsider's reading. A fabulous time is had by all.

Table Etiquette Tips

Table manners have evolved over the centuries. For example, it was once considered polite to pour your tea into the saucer and slurp it, but I don't suggest you try doing that at The Ritz! On the other hand, you shouldn't get so hung up over doing the right thing that you miss out on enjoying the food, drink, and conversation. As I mentioned, the point of practicing good table manners is to show consideration and respect for others. Unless you have been invited to take tea with the Queen, most people will forgive occasional slip-ups. Here are a few pointers:

- If you are not going to do tea leaf reading at the party, and therefore are able to use milk and sugar, put them into the cup first before pouring the tea.

- Hold your teacup with your thumb bent, lacing your index finger through the handle. If you lift your pinkie, you're overdoing it.

- Lift the saucer and cup together when you take tea at a low table. Bring the cup to your lips at the last possible moment to avoid spills.

- Take food from the left and pass to the right.

- Swallow your food before drinking the tea, and then converse. Now you understand the subtle reason Afternoon Tea supplies finger food—it is easier to manage small bites while at the same time you are trying to keep up a conversation and balance a delicate china cup.

- After you use a spoon, knife, or fork, do not set the utensil back down on the table. Place the fork to the left side of the plate, and the spoon and knife to the right.

- When eating a scone, first spread on the jam, then the cream or curd.

- Don't forget to regale your guests with amusing tidbits of history and lore that you've gathered elsewhere in this book.

Teahouses around the World

Whenever I travel for business or pleasure, I make a point of stopping by at least one teahouse. It's always satisfying and relaxing, and it somehow links me into the culture. I pick up ideas on tea and food pairing, presentation, decoration, manners, and customs to enrich my own parties back home. Here are some of my favorite haunts.

Brown's Hotel
Albermarle Street, Mayfair
London, England

My number one preferred place to take Afternoon Tea is at Brown's in London, the hotel Agatha Christie used as the setting for her murder mystery *At Bertram's Hotel*. Evidently the Tea Guild agrees, for it gave the English Tea Room at Brown's the "Top London Afternoon Tea" award in 2009. The hotel's website claims that this longstanding British institution is practiced with sophistication and classic English style. It neglects to mention that the tearoom is one of the coziest and friendliest in the world. The staff goes out of their way to treat the guests kindly and with respect. With the baby grand piano tinkling in the background, the diner has nineteen teas from which to choose. And there's a seemingly endless supply of succulent finger sandwiches and scones with clotted cream and strawberry jam, as well as a variety of delicate pastries and scrumptious cakes from the trolley. The English Tea Room at Brown's is always offering something new and exciting for the tea lover, like the series of "Tea-torials" given by their head pastry chef, Fabien Ecuvillon, wherein participants can create melt-in-your-mouth scones and pastries. A unique recent addition is a "Tea-tox Healthy Afternoon Tea" which includes healthful delights such as hummus and guacamole with crudités; apple and cucumber jelly; low-fat, sugar-free cakes; and sandwiches made with pear, walnut, chicory leaf, poached salmon, mackerel, beets, egg whites, and spelt bread. Still, the Rose Champagne tea remains my favorite.

The Willow Tearooms
Buchanan and Sauchiehall Streets
Glasgow, Scotland

These two Art Nouveau establishments were designed in the early 1900s by world-renowned architect Charles Rennie MacIntosh. He created everything from the structure of the buildings, stained glass windows, color scheme, and black, high-backed chairs to the smallest details of the teaspoons and even the waitresses' dresses. The overriding theme of willow trees (*sauchiehall* is Scottish Gaelic for "alley of the willows") can be seen and appreciated everywhere. The tearooms serve a full dining menu with an inventive tea selection. One of the most intriguing, Summer Pudding Tea, is made from black tea, red currants, raspberries, and strawberries. Yum!

Confeitaria Colombo
Rua Gonçalves Dias
Rio de Janeiro, Brazil

When I lived in Rio, I made a point of stopping by this charming establishment almost daily for lunch or tea. The confeitaria is located in the heart of downtown, away from the crowded beaches. The turn-of-the-century atmosphere of this enchanting belle époque café and teahouse conjures up images of soirées, called *tertúlias* in Portuguese, where the literary giants of nineteenth-century Brazil once gathered. The mahogany woodwork, gigantic polished Belgian mirrors, and dazzling green-and-blue-tinted Art Nouveau stained glass ceiling show Old Rio at its most gracious. I confess my favorite menu item is not the good and plentiful tea, but rather the cream of *palmito*—heart of palm—soup. I can still remember its rich, silky-smooth texture and flavor. The *empanadas*—savory little pies filled with meat, chicken, cheese, or vegetables—are out of this world and the tea is excellent, too.

Dushanbe Teahouse
13th Street
Boulder, Colorado, USA

As a tea lover, I consider myself lucky, as I don't have to travel more than a few blocks in my hometown of Boulder to enjoy taking tea at one of America's largest and most elegant tearooms. Set in the center of this gateway city to the Rockies, like a jewel in a mountain peak crown, the restaurant is a gift to Boulder from our sister city, Dushanbe, the capital of Tajikistan. This small country in central Asia and former member of the Soviet Union, sits along the trade route of the famed Silk Road. The handmade, decorative elements of the teahouse reflect centuries-old Persian design motifs. Over forty artisans created the hand-carved and hand-painted ceiling, plaster carved walls, carved columns, and external ceramic panels that offer a glimpse into the lavish Persian Empire. After being constructed in Tajikistan, the teahouse was dismantled, crated, and shipped to Boulder for reassembly. In central Asia, teahouses serve as community gathering places where friends meet to socialize over a cup of tea and read each other's leaves. In Boulder, the Dushanbe provides the same function.

Wufu Teahouse
Beijing, China

A short list of famous teahouses would not be complete without mentioning this fashionable chain of teahouses in Beijing, China. The name means "Five Kinds of Happiness." Happiness, indeed, is stepping back in time over the celadon flagstone floor into one of these traditional tearooms. Here, patrons relax from the hustle-bustle of modern life in a tranquil ambience surrounded by intricately carved, wooden antique furniture. You can literally drink in the serenity and refined sentiments of the Chinese Gongfu tea ritual poured from exquisite, purple clay teapots.

———

Now that I've told you everything I know about tea divination and more, it's time to turn to some intriguing aspects of tea. In the next chapter, I relate some superstitions associated with this drink and share tips on what to do with all those spent tea leaves you've been accumulating.

seven

Magic of Tea

If man has no tea in him, he incapable of
understanding truth and beauty.

— JAPANESE PROVERB

One of my earliest memories is of my grandparents' tea-making samovar. Bright and shiny, because Grandma polished it weekly, it looked enormous to my child eyes. This mini stove, ensconced on the middle of the dining room sideboard, overwhelmed the space.

Day and night throughout the seemingly endless, gray Great Lakes winters, my grandmother kept the fire stoked under the samovar's hot water tank. The little pot of concentrated tea, kept warm on top of the tank, was diluted with boiling water before drinking. When Grandma poured, hot water sent up billows of steam that fogged the windowpanes and banished the chill from the frigid air. Whenever I wandered into that room, I pretended the samovar was a big, friendly dragon that greeted me by emitting clouds of smoke from its mouth, the tea spout. To my mind, the dark, fragrant, full-bodied brew served in gilded glasses with lemon and a lump of sugar to hold between my teeth composed the lifeblood of this affable beast that warmed and nourished us all.

Tea's almost magical power to wrap me in its steamy, protective mantle and feed my spirit persisted throughout my youth and into adulthood. Tea and herbal infusions saw me through childhood illnesses and helped heal me. When I went off to college where high-quality loose-leaf tea was not available or affordable, I toughed it out by dunking Lipton teabags into Styrofoam cups brimming with scalding water. I drank teabag tea prepared in that way to stay alert while I hit the books. When studying was over and my group of friends, to whom I was known as the teabag reader, gathered to discuss world politics and solve life's problems, mugs of the reviving brew animated us late into the night. On the evening I met my future husband on a basketball court, we adjourned after the game to the student union to share a pot of tea—the first of many.

Tea has attended important moments in my life, cheering me at weddings and births, consoling me after suffering a death in the family. I have drunk tea to lose weight, clear my complexion, boost my immune system, and enhance my performance as a long-distance jogger. Now I'd like to pass along some of the magic I've discovered in tea.

The Legendary "Froth of Liquid Jade"

Did you know that more people worldwide drink tea than coffee? In fact, it is the second most popular drink, surpassed only by water. This is largely due to the huge populations of countries like China and India, where tea is the beverage of choice. With so many people imbibing tea worldwide over so much time, it's no wonder many legends have developed around the drink. To find out more about the fascinating (and sometimes infamous) history of tea, read appendix A.

Given the intriguing stories surrounding tea, it should come as no surprise that in contemporary society it is touted as a miracle brew. Never would I have thought I'd live to see the day when some hardened coffee-drinker friends of mine would switch to my favorite beverage, but to my immense surprise, it has happened. Everyone from aging baby boomers eager to turn back the clock, to Gen-Xers struggling to preserve their youth, to twenty-somethings setting trends with their tea martinis and tea art have embraced tea.

This brings me to the biggest secret I have uncovered about tea: it is, at least in my opinion, the ultimate chameleon. Tea seems to possess an infinite capacity to adapt to consumers of all ages and socioeconomic and cultural backgrounds over almost every era of human history, including this one. I like to think of it as the friendly drink, for it seems to bring people together in harmony.

Tea Superstitions

A beverage so revered in many cultures would not have made it to modern times without a host of associated superstitions and old wives' tales. Here are some funny, outlandish, and fanciful notions about tea to entertain your inquirers, family, and friends.

- Two people should never pour from the same pot or a calamity may strike. If two women pour, one will give birth within a year.
- If a woman allows a man to pour a second cup for her, she will soon fall under his spell.
- Two spoons inadvertently left side by side on the same saucer foretell a wedding within a year.

- A teaspoon dropped on the floor by mistake while taking tea predicts a baby on the way for somebody in the gathering. And you're cheating if you do it on purpose!

- You'd best take heed of how to brew a perfect pot of tea from chapter 2, for if you prepare it too weak, superstition dictates you will lose a friend. On the other hand, if you make it strong, a new friend will appear on the scene. If you get really lazy and forget to boil the water altogether, you can expect several strangers to show up at your door, probably begging for tea.

- If, from the last point, you find the idea of a stranger at your door an intriguing proposition, leave the lid off the pot and see what happens.

- Adding milk to the cup before you put in sugar bodes ill for your love relationships. Luckily, you can avoid that pitfall by taking your tea black.

- Stirring tea in the pot whips up trouble and strife.

- Remember how in chapter 2 you learned that bubbles floating on top of the cupful of tea mean money on the way? You can increase your chances by scooping up the bubbles with a spoon and removing them without touching the sides of the cup. Bring the spoon to your mouth. If you manage to swallow the bubbles before they burst, a letter with good news—or at the very least, a lucky e-mail—will appear soon.

- Some ocean fishermen believe that if they empty the teapot before setting out to sea, the fish will not bite. Worse, if the family empties the teapot before the fishermen leave, the men may be doomed at sea. It seems prudent to me that if you're going fishing, you might stick to coffee.

Twenty Green Uses for Tea

To my mind, part of tea's enchantment lies in its versatility. So far, we have only considered tea in tea leaf reading, but these magical little leaves serve other purposes, too. If you've ever wanted to know what to do with all those spent leaves after you read them besides throwing them into the trash or the garbage disposal, think green with the following suggestions:

- Combine black tea leaves with sage for a superior hair rinse for dark-colored hair.

- Wash your face in cooled black tea to cool sunburn pain. The tannins in tea also help cure mouth ulcers, sore throats, and nipples tender from breast feeding.

- Wash your face in warm tea to eliminate acne and open blocked pores.

- Cold black or chamomile teabags laid on the eyelids are recommended as an analgesic for conjunctivitis (pinkeye). They also rejuvenate tired, puffy eyes.

- Add salt and lemon to a black tea foot bath to alleviate fungal infections, sores, aches, and swelling. While you're at it, bathe the family dog's paws in strong black tea to soften the pads. Soak your own feet (or your teenaged son's, if you can catch him) for twenty minutes in a peppermint tea foot bath to rid them of stinky gym-shoe odor.

- Green teabags placed on allergic skin reactions, such as sweat rash, fever blisters, mosquito bites, or jellyfish stings, lessen pain and itching.

- Strong black tea acts as an antiseptic, so you can use it to help heal small skin lacerations like paper cuts.

- To refresh your carpet, sprinkle on nearly dry, spent tea leaves. Allow them to dry completely, and sweep them up. Who needs all those chemical carpet fresheners?

- If you have ever tried unsuccessfully to rub a tea stain from your favorite tablecloth, you understand its potency as a dye. Lace, net curtains, stockings, paper, and plastic all take this natural dye well.

- Burn tea leaves in the outdoor grill or iron pot on the patio to chase away mosquitoes.
- Chew the leaves to eliminate bad breath or alleviate toothache pain.
- Put used tea leaves in a small bowl and set it in the refrigerator to absorb odors.
- Don't throw away the spent leaves from the teapot after dinner, especially if you have eaten fish or chopped onions. Instead, place your smelly hands in a bowlful of warm water into which you have placed the spent leaves, and soak them for a few minutes.
- You can also fill an accidentally burned saucepan with some spent leaves, salt, and hot water. Let the pan soak overnight to help remove the charred residue.
- Use damp, black tea leaves as a furniture polish.
- Drop the leaves into your compost pile to enrich it.
- Fertilize camellias, roses, and peppers with the spent leaves.
- In some Asian cultures, people eat tea leaves steamed or boiled as a vegetable.

- Cure food in the smoke from smoldering leaves.
- Use tea leaves as an ingredient in breads, soups, sauces, and ice cream.

Finally, for a unique and tasty tea experience, try wearing tea on your lips. Many natural cosmetics companies are beginning to use tea in their lip balms and glosses.

Having Your Tea and Eating It, Too

Writing the end of the last section on tea-flavored lip balms has piqued my appetite to explore how to enjoy tea as food. As some anonymous pundit once said, "Bread and water can so easily be toast and tea." Eating tea is just one more use for this versatile botanical that you may not have thought of, so I end this part of the book with some tea food thoughts.

When tea was introduced to the British Isles in the seventeenth century, people were not quite sure what to do with it. Finally, some women decided to boil the leaves and serve them like spinach. When they learned that tea was meant to be brewed and drunk and the leaves discarded, everyone made fun of the housewives' silly blunder. People shouldn't have laughed.

Tea has been consumed as a food in Asia for 3,000 years. According to an article translated from Chinese by Professor Eric Cazdyn of the University of

Toronto, when you drink a cup of tea, you only ingest the water-soluble nutrients. The other beneficial ingredients, which amount to as much as two-thirds of the tea's nutritive value, remain in the leaves. If you throw them into the garbage, you miss out on the fiber, vitamin E, carotene, protein, and much of the chlorophyll.

An Intercultural Gastronomical Experience

Cooking with tea is an exciting intercultural gastronomical experience, for tea is eaten in unique ways around the world. In Tibet and Mongolia, chefs crush and shape steamed leaves into a cake, then boil it with milk, rice, salt, ginger, orange peel, onion, and spices for a hearty soup. The Burmese prefer to pack their tea with the exotic zaungya fruit and set it aside. After a couple of weeks, they dress the pickled tea with sesame oil. Then they prepare a dish with it made from fried garlic, roasted peas, coconut, peanuts, toasted sesame seeds, and powdered shrimp.

Ochazuke, a kind of tea soup that hails from Japan, is considered a healthy comfort food in much the same way many Americans view chicken soup. The Japanese drink it late at night, by itself for lunch, or after eating a heavy meal, in addition to when they're craving "Mom's comfort food." True green tea masters that they are, the Japanese avail themselves of tea as an ingredient in many common commercial products, from ice cream to bread, gum, candy, cakes, broths, sauces, and marinades. They love the green tea taste so much that they often toss some leaves into a wok with cooking oil and toast them lightly before adding other stir-fry ingredients.

The Chinese also create delicious tea soups and eat tea in sauces and marinades poured over beef and chicken. They smoke food in the leaves, too. Szechuan duck is a famous dish smoked over a mixture of Chinese black tea, sugar, and rice.

What's New under the Teahouse Roof?

With the booming interest in both tea and Asia, it's no wonder fusion and gourmet chefs, not to mention gourmands and the general public, are rediscovering the joys of cooking with and eating tea. The Republic of Tea sells a trans-fat-free stir-fry tea oil for wok frying concocted with extra virgin olive oil. Besides stir-frying with tea oil, tea chefs make ice cream from green, jasmine, and lemon tea, and bake tea along with dried fruit into breads, scones, and Chai crème brulées. My personal favorite confections are delicious Earl Grey and Jasmine chocolate creams.

Teetotaling? Not!

One of the trendiest ways to take tea is in a cocktail. ZEN Green Tea Liqueur, produced by the Suntory group of Japan, is a perfect example. This company is cashing in on the desire of the well-heeled consumer to indulge in alcohol, but at the same time slim down, lower cholesterol, quaff some antioxidants, and perhaps also bring a little peace, harmony, and cheer to after-work relaxation. At around $30 per bottle, the sweet, forest-green-colored liqueur is intended as a premium cocktail ingredient in "Zentinis" and "Zentonics" in the same way that drinkers might sip the popular melon-flavored Midori. This liqueur, however, is concocted from neutral spirits infused with powdered green tea, herbs, lemongrass, and sugar.

For those adventurers who want to try a non-liqueur tea in their alcoholic drinks, bartenders at big-city nightspots are shaking cocktails stirred up from green, black, and scented tea infusions. Such inventions sport zesty names like Green Tea De Lite, Earl Grey marTEAni, and Moroccan Mojito.

I asked renowned tea chef Lenny Martinelli of the Dushanbe Teahouse for his opinion of tea liqueurs. He indicated that in these kinds of cocktails, the subtle taste of tea would probably be obliterated by the strong alcohol flavor. According to Martinelli, even the taste of tea after cooking it is often greatly reduced. When he constructs his own tea dishes—more than forty in all—he aspires to re-create the general idea of a specific tea's taste within the parameters of the culinary flavors of an ethnic cuisine. For example, he'll enhance an Indian tea dish with the typical spices used in Indian cooking and pair it with an appropriate tea drunk in that culture like Darjeeling, Assam, or Chai.

Does all this sound so scrumptious that you're ready to run to the kitchen, tie on the apron, and start baking luscious tea dishes? If so, here's what you need to know.

It's in the Bag: Teabag Cooking

Using teabags may present some advantages over loose leaves. If you don't want to go to the trouble of straining off the leaves, teabags make a no-fuss alternative for soup bases, sauces, and marinades. You can also break open the bags and use the tea inside to season foods in much the same way as you might sprinkle on a spice. Since the leaves in bags are very finely cut, more nutrients are released into the food as an added benefit.

Tea prepared for cooking is stronger than beverage tea. To brew one cup of culinary tea from bags, place two or three bags into a pre-warmed pot and pour 1¼ cups of boiling water over them. Cover the pot and infuse for a couple of minutes, then discard the bags.

Loose-Leaf Cooking

On the other hand, Chef Martinelli advises against using teabags because they contain the smallest, broken parts of the leaf and are not composed of the highest quality tea. He prefers to infuse loose leaves and chop them for a superior flavor and quality. To infuse leaves in a teapot for cooking, place 1 teaspoonful of leaves in the pre-warmed pot and add ½ cup of boiling water. Cover and infuse long enough for the leaves to unfurl. This will render 1 tablespoon of infused leaves for cooking. Refrigerate the leftover liquid to use in a sauce or marinade.

Eating Tea Leaves

At last, we return to the story mentioned previously in this chapter about the seventeenth-century British country housewives who mistakenly cooked the leaves like spinach. These ladies weren't so clueless after all. It turns out that people in Asia have been preparing tea leaves in this way for centuries, and tea leaves are as nutritious and delicious as any vegetable. If you want to test this statement and feel audacious, try stir-frying the leaves in hot sesame oil in a nonstick pan. Or use a designer wok cooking oil.

Cook only for a few seconds until the leaves release their fragrance.

You can also steam the leaves. Place one teaspoonful of leaves in a steamer and steam on high heat for ten minutes to soften the leaves. This will render approximately one-half tablespoon of steamed leaves that you can add to other dishes.

Food and Tea Pairing

As all things old have a way of becoming new again, so tea enthusiasts have once more embraced the age-old Asian custom of pairing food and tea. The next time you host a dinner party, consider planning your menu around tea food and pairing. The following chart gives some of ideas for where to start. The rest is up to you and your creative culinary muse.

Type of Food—Suggested Teas

Seafood, Hawaiian poke—Japanese green teas, like Sencha, Bancha, and Genmaicha, or oolongs

Scallops, lobster, crab—lightly oxidized oolongs

Duck, grilled foods—full and medium oxidized oolongs

Red meats, bacon, smoked salmon sandwich, fatty foods, Stilton cheese, and lemon sorbet—puerhs, Lapsang, English Breakfast, Assam

Chocolate—Darjeeling, Earl Grey

Poultry—Nilgiri, Yunnan, and Keemun

Cucumber or tomato sandwiches, lemon tart, and cheddar cheese—Ceylon Black

Vegetables—pan-fried teas, oolongs

Green salads—Ginger peach blacks

Many cheeses and sausages—Nilgiri, Darjeeling

Pasta with cream sauce—Darjeeling

Pasta with red sauce—Keemun

Pâté, crème brulée, Leicester cheese—Earl Grey

Cream cheese sandwiches, cream desserts—Darjeeling

Many desserts—fruity, berry- and citrus-based teas, Chai

Ice Cream—Tahitian vanilla, jasmine, and passion fruit

————

After stuffing yourself like a goose eating all that tea, you can assuage your guilty feelings by reading about tea's health benefits in appendix B. In the meantime, I hope you'll continue honing your skills in reading the leaves. To that end, the second part of this book gives you clues to decipher the meanings for many of the images you may encounter. As that famous Lapsang Souchong drinker Sherlock Holmes once said, the game's afoot!

Part II

eight

Introduction to the Interpretation of Symbols

*I believe it to be true that dreams are the true
interpretation of our inclinations; but there is
art required to sort and understand them.*

—MONTAIGNE, *Essays II, xii*

Montaigne's words are equally accurate for reading tea leaf symbols. As with any art, interpreting symbols requires some talent, a lot of practice,
and a few basic guidelines. The guidelines for tea
leaf reading are the meanings that have developed
around symbols, and the second part of this book
helps you understand them both. A good memory
is useful, but not necessary. If you get stuck, simply
look up the meanings for the pictures you see in the
cup. The more readings you do, the more readily you
will remember the symbols and their significances.

If you can't find a symbol in this book or the definition given doesn't make sense with regard to the other images you see, ask yourself what the figure means to you. The symbol may also carry a special significance for your inquirers, so remember to ask for their take on images that puzzle you. Remember that a depiction doesn't always have to be symbolic; you can interpret it literally. Some images will look very much like other images, and you might wonder how you can tell the difference between, for instance, a box and a square. Study nearby symbols for clues to meaning and use your intuition.

Instead of listing page after discouraging page of alphabetized symbols that are difficult to sift through, I divide this part of the book into chapters according to type of symbol. With the exception of the final chapter on the zodiac, each is short. You should have no trouble going to the chapter on animals, for example, and immediately finding the information you need for the entry under "Camel." Another advantage to organizing the symbols by chapters is to aid memorization. Even though it is not necessary to learn by heart all these meanings to give a good interpretation, if you are so inclined, you can tackle this enormous task in manageable chunks, one chapter at a time.

The final chapter gives more extensive information on zodiac signs that may appear in the cup. If you know your inquirer's birth sign, you can tailor the reading to fit the particular concerns of those born under the sign, and also expand a birthday reading. Given the parameters of this book, what I say about the astrological signs is not exhaustive. If you are interested in astrological interpretations, I suggest you read a good book on astrology.

Special Symbols for Tea Leaf Reading

Here are some symbols that tend to turn up frequently in teacups and which hold specific meanings in tea leaf reading.

Arrow—A message. (See also **arrow** entry in chapter 24.)

Blobs—If **thick** and chunky, warning of a lawsuit; if **long** and uneven, disappointment.

Clock—May foretell a serious illness where immediate action is required. If the clock is at the rim, it is a good sign for improving health and finances. If it occurs in the middle of the cup, the patient will recover; if at the bottom, the patient may not recover, or the illness will be long-lasting. On the other hand, it may simply remind the inquirer that now is the time to act. If the hands point to 12, a secret rendezvous for love or profit or with an influential person is in the offing.

Cross—One for protection; two for a long life; three for a great achievement. In another tradition, a cross means hardships, burdens, or other troubles. Different schools of interpretation are contradictory, as is the human psyche.

Dashes—Period of thrills and excitement; movement in finances, whether up or down depends on the direction of the dashes; advice to follow through on projects.

Dots—Money, security. A single dot coupled with another symbol emphasizes its meaning.

Drops of water or teardrops—Tears will be shed.

Lines—If **wavy**, a warning or uncertainty; if **parallel**, a spiritual journey, a change in the inquirer's situation; if **straight** and clear, progress, trips; if **slanting downward**, business failure; if **slanting upward**, business success.

Question mark—The outcome of the situation or answer to the question is uncertain. Don't confuse this with the symbol for the asteroid Ceres, which has an entirely different meaning, as explained in chapter 27.

Sticks—A **long** stick may stand for a man; a **short** one, for a woman or child. If they are

parallel, it indicates positive change and that the inquirer is on the right path. If **bent**, the stick signifies hesitation. When it forms a **straight line**, a happy life, accomplishment, and progress are in store for the inquirer. **Several short, straight sticks** indicate illness. If a **forked** stick appears, a decision must be made. (Also see the entry under Y in chapter 20.) Crossed sticks or an X point to an argument or a parting of the ways.

Streak—This formation, which may also look like a dust cloud, bodes a rough time ahead for the inquirer.

Positive and Negative Signs

To help you judge whether a cup is generally positive or negative, here are some common signs. For other positive and negative signs, please look them up individually in the chapters that follow.

Positive—acorn, anchor, angel, bee, beetle, birds flying upward, candle, cherries, cigar, circle, clover, crown, daffodil, diamond, dolphin, eagle, egg, fairy, fir tree, flower, garland, grapes, harp, hen, horse, house, ladder, ladybug, leaf, nest, oak tree or leaf, oar, palm tree, pear, phoenix, pig, pineapple, pinecone, pyramid, rainbow, ribbon, rose, seahorse, shell, shoe, spider, spoon, star, sun, swan, torch, tree, vine, waterfall, well, wings, wishbone.

Negative—acrobat, alligator, axe, bed, bird of prey, clock, clouds, coffin, comet, dagger, feather, glove, goat, gun, hill, hourglass, knife, lightning, lobster, mask, monkey, monster, mouse, nail, needle, pan, rat, rock, saw, scissors, shark, skeleton, skull, teardrops, weapon, willow, wreath.

Theme-Reading Symbols

If your inquirer asks you to read the cup for a specific reason—for example, the person wants to know whether an inheritance will come through, if a lover will ever return, or whether a beloved parent will pass away soon—here are some of the symbols likely to crop up. Again, for more extensive explanations, please refer to the chapters that follow. To boost the information forthcoming in a theme reading, you might want to keep some theme teas handy, as I discussed in chapter 1, such as peppermint for money, chamomile for success, and rose for love.

Career, work—games, sports equipment.

Health—bat, dolphin, fish, lily, machine, vehicle.

Legal issues—shark, skeleton.

Love—flower, heart, ring, the number 10, bouquets, garland, necklace, yoke, diamond, horse's head, crescent.

Luck—triangle, star, clover, crown, star, angel, arch, bird, bamboo, fruit, pig, number 7, frog.

Messages—wings, oblong shape, extended hand, bird in flight, airplane, telephone, arrow, rider on horseback, walking man, candle, fish, comet, letter.

Money, prosperity—cattle, cornucopia, dot, duck, fruit, garden, cluster of grapes, loaf of bread, oak tree, pheasant, jewels, donkey.

Travel, leisure—modes of transportation, map of a region, scenery and landscapes, wings.

Wish fulfillment—arch, group of three triangles, number 9, rising sun, wishbone.

Note on Death

Beginning readers sometimes worry that if they see a very bad sign in the cup such as a skull, it will foretell somebody's death. In spite of the traditional death meanings for symbols that you will find in some symbol books, in my experience, negative symbols never refer to physical death. A skeleton, for example, may mean an illness or poverty. A bat could stand for misfortune or treachery, but never physical death.

Symbols for death can appear in the cup, but not in the way you might think. Cosmically speaking, death is not considered a negative experience; it is simply a transition from one state of being to another. Often a teacup will exhibit positive signs to indicate a person's passing. For example, I once read a cup where the inquirer asked about when her very ill mother would die. Instead of coming up with scythes, owls, bats, crows, and skulls and crossbones, the cup showed a rainbow with birds flying upward. Within the week, my client's mother made a peaceful passage in her sleep, flying over the rainbow, as it were. So there is no need to fear that the cup you read will foretell an actual death in negative terms; I can assure you that it never will.

Animals

In general, animals are good signs, especially for lovers. Farm animals usually presage glad tidings about money. On the other hand, a wild beast may reveal that the inquirer is anxious about something or that misfortune is brewing. Animals are almost always interpreted symbolically unless they are domestic animals, such as dogs or cats. Even in those cases, the interpretation is usually symbolic.

Native Americans may have completely different symbolic interpretations for animals than people from Western societies of European origin. Only a few of such meanings are included here. If you feel especially drawn to things Native American, I suggest you read a good book on Native American symbolism. One of my favorites is the classic *Medicine Cards: The Discovery of Power Through the Ways of Animals* (Jamie Sams and David Carson, Bear and Company, 1988). Along the same lines, Asian animal symbolism can differ radically from Western interpretations. For instance, in Western cultures, the rat is considered dirty, thieving, and prevaricating. In the Chinese zodiac, however, the rat holds an esteemed place as the first of the signs for its intelligence, powers of observation, creativity, and hardworking nature.

Symbolic associations for animals can be very personal, and you never know what a person's totem animal may be. (A totem refers the animal spirit that watches over the person, or from which the individual's ancestors hail.) If you see an animal in a cup, ask your inquirer if it holds a special meaning before attempting an interpretation.

> **Alligator**—treachery, rivals, secret enemies. If the image looks like a **crocodile**, interpret it as indicative of fury.
>
> **Ant**—achievement, perseverance, thrift. Hard work brings gain.
>
> **Bat**—protection, long life, a wish fulfilled; alternatively, a false friend, plots, warning to

weigh words and deeds carefully. Many bats promise great happiness.

Bear—obstacles; danger as the result of a bad decision; an awkward person. Alternatively, a bear could refer to a reassuring person. If the figure is turned away from the handle, it may mean a long trip or delay.

Bee—domestic bliss; good news; a busy time; monetary gain; near the handle, a successful gathering, success at work. A **swarm of bees** indicates public success, a small business, or attendance at a conference or seminar.

Beehive—prosperity, especially in business; activity; creativity.

Beetle—In ancient Egypt, the beetle, or **scarab**, was an important symbol of transformation and creation. It also stands for fortitude and eternal life. A difficult task requiring perseverance will turn out well. The inquirer is following the Path of Light; that is, the spiritual path of true knowledge, clear perception of the truth, and understanding achieved by practicing meditation and harnessing the intuitive mind.

Buffalo—abundance, generosity, courage, survival.

Bull—creativity, fertility, strength, fortitude, machismo, an enemy, quarrels, stubbornness, the zodiac sign Taurus, a father figure.

Butterfly—resurrection, domestic harmony, good luck, silly but enjoyable pastimes, scattered thoughts. If surrounded by dots, the inquirer will spend money on frivolous items or pursuits.

Camel—useful news, fortitude, burdens to bear.

Cat—psychic development, a link with the occult, hidden wisdom, striving for independence, a jealous enemy or false friend. In Chinese symbolism, a **seated cat** brings good luck.

Caterpillar—significant life changes, transformation.

Cattle—prosperity.

Claw—enemies, advice against taking risks.

Cow—beauty, creation, fertility, motherhood, childbirth, endurance, patience, the zodiac sign Taurus.

Coyote—Beware of tricks being played.

Crab—enemies, period of ill humor, separation, the zodiac sign Cancer.

Cricket—good luck.

Deer—gentleness, a time for nurturing.

Dog—faithful friend; protection in matters of law and finance; one's "guiding light"; if **barking**, advice from a friend; if **howling**, an unhappy event. **Many dogs** stand for a get-together of friends.

Dolphin—safe journey, help offered in an emergency. The inquirer is rewarded for past actions.

Donkey—patience, pride, inheritance, good luck.

Dragonfly—fantasy, pleasure. Beware of self-delusion.

Elephant—a trusted friend; wisdom; strength; long-lasting success; a long journey, either in the mind or physically; something to do with the nations of India or Thailand.

Fish—salvation; good fortune, money, success; marital happiness, fertility; a Christian, or something to do with Christianity; invitation to a meal; felicitous meeting with someone from abroad; the zodiac sign Pisces. The inquirer will lead a charmed life. **Several fish** bode disappointment.

Fly—depression, illness, a pesky annoyance.

Fox—a cunning, deceitful person; shrewdness, especially in business.

Frog—fertility, pregnancy, success and happiness through a change of job or home. If the image looks like a **toad**, the meaning changes to "evil forces at work."

Giraffe—distortion of a situation.

Goat—news from a sailor, an enemy, the zodiac sign Capricorn. Something is bothering the inquirer.

Grasshopper—news from a friend away on travels, advice against scattered interests, a sticky situation, plague.

Hare—timidity, news from a friend, marriage; fertility. A crisis needs quick, bold decisions and actions in order to be averted.

Horse—By tradition, a **horse's head** means the appearance of a lover. A **galloping** horse brings good news; a man on a horse transports money. A **horseshoe** signifies good luck. Horses hold different significances for various cultures. They can personify both fire and light, but sometimes are taken to foreshadow death and destruction.

Kangaroo—domestic harmony; alternatively, unsettling times; something to do with the nation of Australia; advice to the inquirer to make a plan and stick to it.

Ladybug—a windfall, fertility, a happy home.

Lamb—a gentle person, something that will happen in the springtime, comfortable material circumstances.

Lion—zodiac sign Leo; ambition, pride; alternatively, regeneration; advice to take immediate action. The inquirer will conquer enemies and prosper, perhaps with the help of an influential friend or relative.

Lizard—treachery; false rumors; alternatively, good luck.

Lobster—financial difficulties; a trip to the seacoast, perhaps to New England or Florida.

Monkey—mischief; self-deception; dangerous flattery; the baser instincts of the unconscious mind; a scandal; alternatively, affection, protection, good health. In Chinese symbolism, a quick and witty mind.

Moth—fatal attraction.

Mouse—financial loss, theft, arguments among family or friends. A quiet, unassuming person will influence the inquirer's life.

Octopus—danger, entrapment, many events occurring at the same time.

Otter—It's time to play and take life at a leisurely pace.

Ox—hard work, often for no recognition; self-sacrifice; the zodiac sign Taurus. Patience is required in a situation that will arise.

Oyster—riches, a long courtship, advice to share one's thoughts with others.

Pig—financial success, but emotional problems; a happy-go-lucky person with a tendency to overeat; a greedy person; alternatively, a banker; the zodiac sign Virgo. The Chinese consider the pig a very lucky sign.

Rabbit—sexual concerns; timidity; adaptability. Something good will occur in the spring.

Ram—aggressive person; alternatively, the zodiac sign Aries. A project gets off to a fast start, but may require a lot of work to see it through.

Rat—double-cross, loss, an unknown enemy.

Scorpion—stinging criticism that strikes to the heart, the zodiac sign Scorpio.

Seahorse—family affairs, a gay male. A gamble waged now will pay off.

Seal—an ambitious person who will do anything to achieve goals.

Shark—difficult dealings with lawyers, material loss, danger.

Snake—Someone who bears a grudge is plotting against the inquirer. A **viper** may also stand for false friends or vicious hatred. Alternatively, it may mean it is time to move on. If the snakes are **entwined**, then the significance changes to "healing" and the medical profession. Some Native American tribes perceive the snake as a sign of renewal.

Spider—an excellent sign, often meaning that fate is at work in a positive way in the inquirer's life; working hand in hand with destiny; good luck; cosmic protection; self-determination; industrious labor. When combined with dots, a spider signifies monetary gain; alternatively, cunning and intrigue.

Squirrel—money saved; advice to streamline one's life.

Stag—a healthy, handsome, virile young man.

Tiger—regions of India, Malaysia, or Siberia. A risk taken will turn out in the inquirer's favor. In Chinese symbolism, the tiger means intimidation, boldness, and a quick temper.

Tortoise—eventual triumph; getting ahead by proceeding with caution; slow but sure progress; alternatively, criticism or obstacles difficult to surmount.

Whale—regeneration, creativity, intuition, success in business, anxiety over nothing. A big project comes to fruition.

Wolf—jealousy; loss; need; intrigue; alternatively, a wise spiritual teacher.

Zebra—secret love affair; an adventure abroad, perhaps to Africa. The inquirer, by choice, becomes a wanderer.

ten

Architecture

An image of a generic building or something that forms part of a building, such as a brick or an archway, can mean that the inquirer is ready to construct a new life or project. Many buildings clumped together in a city landscape can stand for a particular city. Edifices dedicated to specialized pursuits may symbolize the specific activity that takes place inside, such as education in a school or finance in a bank.

Abbey/ Monastery/Convent—Buildings of this type, cloistered away from the modern world, stand for a desire to seek refuge. On the other hand, they may indicate a period of rest from daily activities and concerns or consolation.

Archway—new projects, roads open, weddings, partnerships, a trip to a faraway destination, good fortune.

Attic—something hidden from the inquirer's conscious mind.

Basement—practical considerations, stockpiled resources, preoccupation with the physical world.

Brick(s)—solid foundation, steady growth of an enterprise or a plan.

Bridge—an opportunity or choice offered; changes.

Castle—wish fulfilled; a happy event; a strong, successful person; security; nobility; equity through marriage; an inheritance.

Church/Temple—sudden financial gain, a ceremony, faith, aspirations, gifts of the spirit, help offered.

Column—journey, a clear path ahead, a promotion, success, warning against arrogance.

Door—opportunity; if **closed**, the opportunity may be ignored.

Fence—constriction, hurdles to jump, success after minor setbacks.

Fountain—life force, sexual energy, joy.

Gate—sudden change in fortune, opportunity. If the gate stands **open**, all is well. If **closed**, the obstacles are of inquirer's making.

House—change of residence or business premises, security, domestic harmony, better times ahead. Businesses started now will succeed.

Pyramid—long-abiding success, spirituality.

Roof—change in location, feelings of vulnerability.

Room—desire for privacy. Family activities take the forefront.

Ruins—Shattered hopes and dreams are followed by a fresh start. If you are familiar with the Tower trump XVI in the tarot, the meaning is similar.

Spire/Steeple—spiritual advancement. The inquirer's fortunes rise to great heights.

Stadium—The inquirer will be the focus of attention and even, perhaps, of public adulation, or will possibly feel like a sidelined spectator of events.

Staircase—spiritual attainment, profound knowledge gained.

Tent—travel, vacation, secrets, a need to get away. The current situation, whatever it may be, is temporary.

Theater—teamwork, fantasy, artifice, manipulation, a gregarious person, a drama queen, a professional actor, a person born under the zodiac sign Leo. This symbol may augur fame and recognition for the inquirer.

Threshold—exciting new changes. Events take a thrilling, unexpected turn.

Tower—either opportunity or disaster, depending on whether it is whole, half-built, or crumbling; advice to be watchful. (See entry under **ruins** for more meanings.)

Wall—misunderstanding, building for the future.

Window—clear vision, unless obscured by clouds. If the window stands **open**, it means good luck comes through a friend or associate. If it remains **closed**, a friend or associate creates disappointment.

Birds

Birds are almost always interpreted symbolically, and usually as positive signs. If flying, they are considered harbingers of good news. Water birds like **herons** and **sandpipers** are always fortunate symbols. An exception is made for **birds of prey**, which usually stand for enemies.

It may be difficult to identify a particular bird in a cup, as they are usually quite small. First, check for the bird's position and determine whether it is flying or at rest. If **flying** at the top of the cup, the bird stands for hopes, ideals, and leadership. If it is flying low in the cup, the inquirer's practical interests will flourish. A **flock of birds** points to a fortunate gathering. A **nesting** bird means good luck and domestic bliss. If **perched**, the significance changes to waiting for good news. Meanings for specific birds follow.

> **Bird quill**—documents to sign, advice to return to a simpler lifestyle.
>
> **Canary**—lover, singer.
>
> **Chicken**—industriousness, successful completion of a project, the comforts of home. An important event will likely occur in the spring.
>
> **Cock, rooster**—something to crow about, pride, arrogance, boastfulness, wealth and financial independence, advice not to hesitate, also advice to weigh one's words before speaking.
>
> **Crane**—long life, love, justice, enlightenment, protection.
>
> **Crow**—something to be proud of, gossip, a message.
>
> **Dove**—peace, tranquility, domestic bliss.
>
> **Duck**—money, fidelity, good luck in speculation, profitable associates abroad.
>
> **Eagle**—opportunity, favorable news, power, fame, triumph over adversity, heightened perceptions, gifts of the spirit, change of resi-

dence. The inquirer will use personal skills to achieve a cherished aim.

Falcon—promotion, success.

Feather—scattered energies, inability to concentrate, instability, inconsistency, unpredictability, an insincere person. In my experience, feathers have the habit of appearing attached to hats or people's heads. In those cases, the meaning may have to do with one of the inquirer's friends, relatives, or associates.

Goose/Geese—unexpected but fascinating guests; an invitation to a social event.

Gull—survival, gullibility.

Hawk—trouble, possibly from a jealous rival, a person with keen symbolic or literal vision.

Hen—birth, domestic bliss, a female visitor, wealth.

Hummingbird—joy, zest for life.

Nest—security, a supportive loving family. If the nest contains eggs, it may refer to children, or perhaps a nest egg.

Ostrich—travel, warning not to shirk responsibilities.

Owl—The owl is one of those symbols considered either all good or all bad, depending on the reader's point of view. For some, the owl represents wise counsel and prophecy, perhaps even a fascinating mystery to be solved. Since these birds are active at night, an owl could refer to a night person or to something that will happen at night. Others associate owls with failure, scandal, or abysmal luck.

Parrot—trip to the tropics, scandal, gossip.

Peacock—riches, an estate, a wealthy marriage, success in the eyes of the world, vanity, pride. If poorly positioned with surrounding negative symbols, a peacock may refer to trouble with heirs.

Pelican—parental devotion.

Penguin—happiness, a trip to the Southern Hemisphere, news from someone living south of the inquirer.

Pheasant—vacation in the countryside, a legacy, a promotion.

Phoenix—rebirth, longevity, domestic tranquility, peace, prosperity, benevolence, empire, fidelity, justice, obedience, rectitude.

Pigeon—love, international travel, news from someone living or traveling abroad.

Raven—message, wisdom, healing, advice against pessimism.

Robin—period of good luck, the end to a troubling situation. An important event will happen in early spring.

Sparrow—mysterious disappearance, improvement in the inquirer's finances.

Stork—birth of a new business or a physical birth.

Swallow—Luck is on the inquirer's side.

Swan—contentment, mysticism, desire fulfilled. A lover may suddenly enter the inquirer's life.

Turkey—good luck in the late fall; a family get-together; an obtuse, badly behaved person; a flop.

Vulture—robbery; danger; loss; enemies in high places; alternatively, protection by those in power.

Wings—Messages arrive speedily and bear good news.

twelve

Body Parts

Body parts, hmm. Sounds gruesome, but if you think in terms of symbols, it really isn't so bad. As you will find in chapter 14—on clothing and personal items—images of human body parts can stand for a person with whom the inquirer associates the particular part. For example, an eye could indicate a financial advisor who will suggest the inquirer sell some stock and switch to a safer investment. A hand might point to a person who makes a living doing manual labor, or to a basketball or baseball player whom the inquirer knows. A body part may also refer to an injury or illness that will affect that area of the inquirer's body.

Arm—offer of help; protection, perhaps from a member of the police force or a security company; if **coupled with a weapon**, danger.

Beard—older man, a deception, or simply a person the inquirer knows who wears a beard.

Bones—health advisory, hunger, environmental toxins, a person born under the zodiac sign Capricorn.

Ear—good news. A positive attitude prevails.

Eye—advice to take heed, or keep an open mind; protection. Someone is watching the inquirer. Psychic ability and intuition will come to the inquirer's aid.

Face—someone whom the inquirer knows. Look to see if the face seems to be smiling, frowning, scowling, frightened, surprised, or looking crafty.

Finger—something that the inquirer needs to notice. Note the image(s) to which it is pointing for clues.

Foot/Feet—important decision, a pilgrimage, good news.

Hand—strength, friendship, charity, union. If the hand is **facing upward**, it may mean a plea for help. If it is **clenched** in a fist, it could refer to a quarrel or miserliness. If it **points downward**, it indicates a failure or fortunes taking a downturn. **Two hands shaking** show a meeting with a stranger who will become important to the inquirer, or alternatively, an agreement or partnerships.

Heart—love, a caregiver; when **broken**, unlucky in love; something that will occur around Valentine's Day; with an **arrow pointing downward**, someone intends to harm the inquirer; with an **arrow pointing upward**, someone will protect the inquirer; with an **arrow straight across**, someone is smitten with the inquirer. This symbol could also indicate psychic self-development or the power of the unconscious mind, depending on nearby symbols. A heart may also indicate physical heart trouble.

Leg—new experience, a step up in life.

Skeleton—illness, poverty. A **skull** stands for secrets that may harm the inquirer if made public. A **skull and crossbones** warns of a rip-off, also emotional or actual poison.

Teeth—aggression, illness.

Thumb—control issues, an artistic person. If two thumbs **point up**, all will be well; if they **point down**, trouble and woe are ahead.

thirteen

Playing Cards

Playing cards may be the most universally recognized set of symbols that exist. Even people who aren't keen on memorizing symbols will probably recognize what the suits mean from having played cards. Then there are those who take up the tarot and study card symbols in depth as a philosophical pursuit. Following is a sample of some of the most common meanings attributed to the suits and various cards. For numbers, such as those that would appear on cards, please see chapter 20. Note that if you recognize the symbol of a suit in a cup—that is, a spade, diamond, heart, or club—it may simply mean that the inquirer will visit a gambling town like Las Vegas or Monaco or a casino on a Native American reservation, or that the person may soon take a risk.

Clubs/Wands/Rods—enthusiasm, new ventures, new people, problems to overcome, travel for pleasure, intellectual creativity, the unconscious mind, business dealings, marketing, good luck with money, great news, money through the mail or computer, a project startup, invention, education, helpful people, good reasons for taking action.

Hearts/Cups—love, emotions, marriage, happiness, joy, creative talents, family, beauty, abundance, productivity, fertility, birth, satisfaction, completion, the past.

Spades/Swords—the intellect, science, reasoning, language arts, troubles, illness, quarrels, separation, endings, swift action, courageousness, creativity, help from professionals, bad luck, sadness, need to seek balance or the end to a situation. If located at the **rim**, the symbol may bode setbacks or disappointments. If at the **bottom**, it points to sorrow, misfortune, endings, or a loss. If the symbol points towards the **rim**, troubles are surfacing; if it points **downward**, troubles will subside.

Diamonds/Pentacles—physical existence, money, stocks and bonds, awards, gifts, protection, good news, a letter or e-mail, property, contracts, possessions, business, finance, large-scale projects, personal values, practical creativity, marriage proposal, business proposition, ring or luxurious gift.

Ace—beginnings, a fortuitous environment, contentment, success, ecstasy, a birth.

King—father figure; a strong-willed, influential, powerful man, committed to achieving his goals.

Queen—mother figure; wife; an influential, powerful woman.

Jack/Knight—message; lover; an independent, active man.

Joker/Clown—trickster, job with the circus, beginnings. The advice offered is not to over-analyze or take oneself too seriously.

Clothing and Personal Items

The items listed in this chapter present a perfect example of how the tea leaves arrange themselves into the little things we buy and use every day to show us images of our hopes and fears, struggles and goals. If the clothes seem brand-new, you can assume the inquirer is moving up in the world. Likewise, if they appear rumpled, old, and/or torn, the person's life is headed for a downturn. You may distinguish clothing for a special occasion, such as a bridal gown or a tuxedo. One way to interpret this example is to say that the inquirer is going to attend a wedding or other formal event.

Hats are especially meaningful and appear frequently in tea leaf readings. If they are associated with a profession, such as a nurse's cap, then a nurse, or someone who will offer help, will become important to the inquirer. A policeman's helmet may indicate protection or security, but it may also portend a run-in with the law, depending on nearby symbols. A mortarboard with a tassel could signify the inquirer's desire to attain higher education, or advice from a wise counselor. A hat can also mean that someone is attempting to hide something from the inquirer or that the inquirer is very busy, as in "wearing many hats."

If the article of clothing is feminine, then the inquirer possesses the ability to charm others or may engage in a flirtation. If the items are masculine in nature, they may refer to sports or professions. Whether the items seen are in a male's or a female's cup, the meaning is the same.

> **Apron**—new friends. The inquirer may feel tied close to home.
>
> **Boot**—divine protection; achievement. If **facing away from the handle**, it could signify a dismissal, movement afoot, or may refer to the nation of Italy. A **pair of boots** stands for protection, travel, or sales made.

Bow—flirtation, a present. Somebody holds the inquirer in high esteem.

Bracelet—marriage proposal, a social gathering, a gift.

Cap—trouble, advice to take heed, discretion advised, warning against speculation.

Coat—separation, end of a friendship, something hidden.

Collar—dependence, constriction, the clergy.

Comb—release from small obligations, a woman.

Crown—well-earned victory. If **very clearly formed**, it could presage a legacy; respect, or honors. If the crown is coupled with **stars**, it is a fortunate symbol of good luck coming out of the blue.

Fan—flirtation, gossip, verbal discretion advised, romance, a party, female eroticism, lunar powers at work.

Glove—challenge, justice meted out, an invitation.

Jewelry—a gift.

Lace—a secret, improvement in the inquirer's life.

Mask—deception; a ball or a party. An important event will occur in February.

Necklace—if **whole**, admirers; if **broken**, a relationship ends.

Pipe—The inquirer is considering an issue; keep an open mind. Or, an older man with the inquirer's best interests at heart.

Purse—a "tightwad." The recommendation is to curb spending. If coupled with **dots**, the inquirer will have enough money to live comfortably.

Ribbons—fulfillment. (See **Bow**, previous page.)

Shirt—Protection, unless appearing hazy, in which case the inquirer will lose money.

Shoe—liberty, independence; positive change, the female sex organs. Delayed news will be positive.

Umbrella—mourning, disappointment, troubles. If **inside-out**, the troubles are of the inquirer's making; if **open**, the inquirer is protected. If the umbrella is **closed**, either no shelter will be found, or it may refer to a paternal figure.

Veil—secret revealed.

fifteen

Common Objects

The familiar items that surround you—household objects, furniture, food you eat, entertainment items—generally indicate domestic tranquility and happiness. Over the past few years, images of computers and smartphones have surfaced more often in the cups I read. These machines have become such an integral part of contemporary life that it's difficult to interpret exactly what they might mean in specific instances. I usually start by asking the inquirer whether, how, and how frequently he or she uses a computer or cell phone. In this way, I am able to narrow the options to job, social networking, creative endeavors, etc. Although there are too many common objects to list, this chapter notes a few that pop up frequently in the teacup.

> **Bag**—surprise, raise, reward or advancement, power. Something important is about to happen. If the bag is **closed**, the inquirer may feel trapped.

> **Ball**—restlessness, fortunes bouncing around like a ball, the inquirer bouncing back from adversity, striding forward, a desire to move, involvement in sports.

> **Balloon**—success in life. Exaggerated troubles will soon pass.

> **Barrel**—party. If **whole**, good fortune or an upturn in finances is rolling toward the inquirer. If **broken**, something is lacking in the inquirer's life.

> **Basket**—recognition, a gift, a baby. If the basket appears at the **top of the cup**, it means wealth or bounty. If **near the handle**, it stands for an actual baby. A **flower-filled** basket highlights social success and excellent health. When coupled with **dots**, money is coming soon.

> **Bed**—possible illness, lack of energy or motivation, sexual thoughts. The counsel is to take a rest or vacation. If the covers appear **rum-**

pled, restlessness is indicated. A **neatly made** bed shows a well-ordered mind.

Bell—announcement; if near the **top**, promotion at work; near the **bottom**, bad news. **Coupled bells** stand for joy; **many bells**, a wedding.

Book—higher learning, studious pursuits, advice, lawsuits. More information is needed before a decision can be made. A **closed** book identifies a secret or the need to acquire a new skill. An **open** book presages success or a pleasant surprise.

Bottle—social invitation, conviviality. If it resembles a **perfume bottle**, the inquirer will revisit happy memories.

Box—a gift. If **open**, romance will prevail; if **closed**, lost property will be recovered. An **oblong** box reveals that the inquirer is hiding something; alternatively, someone is hiding something from the inquirer. (See more meanings under **square** in chapter 17.)

Bread—prosperity, abundance. The inquirer's labors will bear fruit.

Broom—beginnings, new home, a fresh start.

Cage—a loveless marriage. The inquirer feels trapped.

Candle—higher education, thirst for knowledge, help offered, an improving situation, inspiration.

Cauldron—fertility, a birth in the family or of an idea.

Chain—engagement, wedding, union, agreement, bonding, successful communication, restrictions. A broken chain shows disappointment. A chain can also mean that a series of events will affect the inquirer's life.

Chair—improving conditions, an unexpected guest, suggestion to rest. If the chair is **empty**, someone leaves the inquirer's life; if **occupied**, someone enters the inquirer's life.

Cigar—a new, influential friend.

Clock—Events having a strong impact on the inquirer's life depend on others and/or the environment in which the person is moving. (See entry in chapter 8 for more meanings.)

Crib—birth of a child, idea, or enterprise. A hope becomes a reality.

Cup/Chalice—reward gained through effort, love, happiness, immortality, a legacy. Positive criticism is being directed toward the inquirer. A **cracked** cup reveals that the inquirer is disappointed in life.

Desk—a task to complete. A letter brings news concerning business or an incident at work.

Dice—warning not to gamble now.

Dish/Plate—domestic spat.

Doll—passing pleasures.

Egg—positive changes, success, fertility, pregnancy, success through planning and hard work, protection.

Fireplace—a happy, prosperous home; good luck.

Flag—victory, danger, quarrels. A flag that looks like a **banner** stands for honors, fame, or a successful marriage.

Fork—flattery, deceit; a decision splits feelings, a choice offered.

Funnel—frustration, slowdown in events.

Glass—integrity.

Hammock—repose, relaxation, release from stress.

Inkpot—contract to be signed, problem solved.

Jug/Pitcher—diversions, radiant health. The inquirer's money situation and reputation improve.

Kite—wish fulfilled, daydreams, a holiday, recommendation to exercise prudence.

Knot—achievement; alternatively, lack of success. A problematic situation has the inquirer feeling tied up in knots.

Lamp—marriage, quest, enlightenment. The inquirer's studies may be interrupted by a stranger who at first will be resented, but later, appreciated. When the lamp appears **near the cup's rim**, it indicates a celebration; if **near the handle**, money. **Two lamps** stand for two marriages.

Oven—pregnancy, as in "a bun in the oven."

Package—a surprise, a gift.

Pail—a need to clear the decks and leave the present situation.

Pan—petty anxieties, accusations, domestic strife.

Pen—written communication. A pen may refer to an author.

Pin—new job.

Pot—magical times ahead. Intuition comes into play.

Spoon—generosity, a birth. **Two spoons** mean a marriage proposal.

Staff—The inquirer will be provided for.

Table—festive gathering, business meeting, abundance, comfort, blessing, hard work.

Teapot—committee meeting, discussions.

Telephone—a message.

Thimble—A domestic scene changes, usually for the better.

Torch—improving conditions; new, enthusiastically tackled interests; spiritual enlightenment. If **poorly aspected**, a torch could reveal a breakup of a love affair from which the inquirer will suffer.

Vase—a friend in need, a secret admirer, good deeds, peace of mind.

Wheel—inheritance, wealth, advancement through personal effort, travel, a promotion, the force of destiny, good fortune, a positive destiny. A wheel **spotted near the rim** refers to unexpected money. A **broken** wheel augurs disappointment; one who is away will return soon.

sixteen

Flowers

Few people fail to feel uplifted by the beauty of flowers. In general, flowers symbolize happiness, joy, prosperity, luck, fulfillment, a carefree period, honors, a wish fulfilled, beauty, springtime, renewal, love, marriage, and compliments from an admirer. A **bouquet** of flowers stands for joy, prosperity, luck, love, and marriage, while a **garland** points to fellowship, honors, success, and marriage. A **wreath** may indicate a funeral, laurels, or an event that will occur near the end of December.

The interpretation of an individual flower depends on many factors, including color, size, shape, and fragrance. Following are meanings for some common flowers that frequently appear in readings. If you want to learn more, I suggest you consult the classic book of Victorian flower meanings, *Language of Flowers* (Margaret Picston, Michael Joseph, Ltd., 1968).

> **Blossoms**—It is difficult to distinguish what kind of tree blossom you are looking at when they appear a cup, but coupled symbols, the inquirer's question and your own intuition may help. Traditional meanings for some blossoms include: **Apple**—preference, motherhood; **Apricot**—a love affair; **Cherry**—a good education; an innocent young woman; Washington, DC; **Peach**—a long life; **Pear**—lasting friendship, comfortable material circumstances; **Plum**—strength in adversity (as the plum is the first tree to put forth blossoms in late winter), a trip to Asia or something to do with Asian art. In the language of flowers, the plum tree stands for loyalty and independence.
>
> **Carnation**—love, a maternal figure.
>
> **Daffodil**—wealth and success, a good friend, hope, chivalry, respect.

Daisy—a blissful, youthful marriage; young love; innocence. A happy event will occur in the spring.

Dandelion—coquetry, a person born under the zodiac sign Leo, pride.

Geranium—gentility.

Heliotrope—devotion.

Honeysuckle—lasting affection.

Iris—purity, romance in a garden, someone named Iris. An intriguing message is about to be transmitted.

Lavender—devotion, cleanliness; the inquirer will be cared for.

Lilac—spring love.

Lily—purity, health, happiness, a funeral. Someone or something passes from the inquirer's life.

Lily of the Valley—trustworthiness, a magical experience, fond childhood memories.

Lotus—fertility, good fortune, femininity, chastity, beauty, eloquence. The lotus is also associated with Eastern religions like Buddhism and Hinduism; hence, it could mean an inclination toward those types of spirituality or a trip to Asia.

Pansy—individual of a thoughtful nature. Somebody is thinking of the inquirer.

Poppy—sleep, imagination, pleasure, peace, wartime remembrances.

Rose—love, perfection, joy, good children, popularity, success in the arts, romance, someone named Rose.

Sunflower—blessings of nature, strength, happiness.

Tulip—passion, something to do with the Netherlands.

Violet—a person named Violet. A walk through the forest (actual or symbolic) will lead to love.

seventeen

Geometric Shapes

Geometric shapes have always held a special allure. A possible reason for this fascination may be the mathematical principles involved creating them, which in ancient times were considered a form of magic. Over time, each shape has taken on special meanings, some of which are related in the following.

> Circle/Ring—completion, good luck. A circle coupled with a dot foretells a pregnancy. If it is cut by lines, it means disappointment,

unfinished business or a delay. A broken circle portends a parting of the ways. If the circle seems like a ring, it could predict a marriage. (See also **sun, moon,** and **ball,** chapters 27 and 15.)

Diamond—prosperity, money, expensive gifts.

Hexagon—protection, Judaism, the truth, manifestation of the will on the material plane. (See also entry under **hexagram,** chapter 23.)

Oblong—a package or a letter. These days, the letter could stand for an important e-mail.

Oval—a female. Beware of self-pride.

Pentagon—triumph of the human spirit over matter, the Wiccan religion, military matters. (See also entries under **pentagram,** chapters 19 and 23.)

Square—tight spot or quandary, hardships, hindrances, protection from accidents, comfort. (See also entry under **box,** chapter 15.)

Triangle—unexpected news; if **pointing upward**, success, or the inquirer is guided by spiritual considerations; if **pointing downward**, failure, or the inquirer is guided by material considerations. It may also refer to a **lovers' triangle.**

eighteen

Musical Instruments

Maybe it's because as children, many of us take lessons on musical instruments or perhaps the ability to play an instrument seems such a highly creative, yet difficult talent to master that instruments appear in readings. Whatever the reason, musical instruments are positive signs, usually indicative of the inquirer's capacities, gifts, and achievements. They also stand for enjoyment of cultural activities. Following are some specifics.

Bagpipe—something to do with Scotland, a blowhard.

Bell—an announcement; **two bells**, a harmonious love affair.

Clarinet—frivolity, communication with spirits from the other side.

Cymbals—praise, worship, a hubbub, a noisy person, insincerity.

Drum—new job, possibly in public life; gossip; quarrels.

Flute—pleasant, profitable meeting; a charming person.

Guitar—gift of music, wining and dining, romance.

Harp—harmony, romance, happiness in marriage, blessings of the spirit.

Horn—an announcement, advice against tooting one's horn.

Orchestra—working in harmony.

Piano—self-expression, solid achievements, period of rock-hard financial stability.

Saxophone—deep connection with another person.

Trombone—Love conquers all.

Trumpet—an announcement of an important event, fame for the inquirer.

Ukulele—something having to do with Hawaii, suggestion to take a seaside vacation and relax.

Violin—individualism, gaiety, egotism, popularity, a musical event.

Xylophone—enhanced communicative abilities. Multitasking skills come into play.

nineteen

Natural and Supernatural Worlds

Vital to people in primitive societies and still important to us today, the atmospheric conditions, everything we see in the sky, the landscape, and the bodies of water that surround us often take on emotionally charged symbolic meanings. These are the oldest forms of divination, and the symbolism is therefore deeply rooted in our subconscious minds. Because these phenomena are large-scale, we often associate them with yearning to get away from our present environments and travel to distant lands, or to engage in a completely different occupation. Following are some signs you may see.

Abyss—dark forces at work. Spiritually speaking, the abyss is the void that must be transcended in order to unite with the godhead.

Anubis—The jackal-headed god of ancient Egyptian myth stands for judgment.

Canyon—Generally, this is an unlucky sign unless the inquirer lives near or is drawn to canyons. For instance, for many who live in the Rocky Mountains, an image of a canyon seen in a cup would probably carry a neutral connotation, such as the inquirer will travel through a canyon to a neighboring town.

Cave—secrets, something hidden from the inquirer. In Jungian symbolism, a cave may refer to a mother figure. It can also represent a miner or a person who works with the earth to create something like ceramics.

Clouds—trouble, doubts, fleeting worries.

Comet—misfortune. Expect the unexpected.

Crescent moon—financial security, yearning for freedom, travel to a faraway land, romance with an exotic stranger, a crossroads in life. The inquirer will achieve success with the help of women. If it looks like a **first quarter** moon, new beginnings are in order. If the symbol appears to be a **last quarter** moon, energy ebbs, fortunes decline, or the inquirer will undergo a period of depression.

Desert—deep understanding, spiritual knowledge.

Dragon—obstacles, challenges, great power, a sudden change, upheaval, good luck, material gain, longevity, something to do with Asia or Wales.

Field/Meadow—great potential, limitless horizons. New business ventures will succeed.

Fire—hasty action or reaction, anger, achievement, passion, a strong reaction to an event, good health.

Fog—confusion, a mystery, something obscured from the inquirer's vision.

Forest—See chapter 26 for information on trees.

Full moon—romance, travel, family, a love affair. (See also **sun** and **circle**, chapters 27 and 17.)

Garden—fertility, the fruit of one's labors, personal growth.

Hill/Mountain—obstacles to surmount, but great achievement is possible. If **traversed by a road**, the inquirer will succeed.

Ice—disapproval, hostility, danger of an accident, the feeling that time or an opportunity is slipping away.

Island—isolation, loneliness, independence, an island nation.

Lake—a mystery.

Lightning—caution to control anger. A sudden event or brainstorm may change the course of the inquirer's life.

Phoenix—rebirth, longevity, domestic tranquility, benevolence, obedience, fidelity, justice, rectitude.

Rain—blessings, fertility; alternatively, depression. If it seems like a **deluge**, the inquirer's property may be destroyed. (See also **dashes**, chapter 8.)

Rainbow—brighter times ahead, prosperity, good luck.

River—The inquirer's most cherished possession will last forever. Alternatively, the inquirer's possessions will be lost; that is, they will "float downriver."

Rock—annoying problems, obstacles; alternatively, stability, a rock-solid relationship, someone involved in the mining industry; the Southwest.

Seascape—travel, movement in the inquirer's affairs, change of residence.

Shell—love, devotion, a comfortable life in the next world, fertility, femininity, good luck, prosperous journeys, a seaside vacation, money coming to the inquirer, a spiritual journey.

Sphinx—The answer is not to be revealed at this time; please ask the question later.

Star/Pentagram—happiness, good fortune, excellent health, providential protection, great good fortune. Small stars **clustered** around the handle point to talented off-spring.

Sun—creativity, happiness, success, growth, honors, a birth, the zodiac sign Leo. Summertime brings happiness to the inquirer's life. (See also entries under **circle** and **moon**, chapters 17 and 27.)

Tempest—Offensive developments.

Unicorn—elopement, chastity, self-sacrifice. A problem is solved or enhanced intuition is on target.

Valley—creativity. Strength of character leads to victory, accomplishment, and peace of mind. A valley may refer to a person who works the land, for example, a farmer.

Volcano—a tense, explosive relationship. A volcano may mean destruction of old plans on which a new foundation will be laid. If you are familiar with the symbolic meanings of tarot's major arcana card XVI, the Tower, a volcano and a tower share similar meanings.

Waterfall—prosperity, love, a challenge.

Wave—pure intentions, vacillation.

Numbers and Letters

Numbers are always significant and usually relate to the symbols surrounding them. Often, they refer to important dates; a number of hours, days, weeks, months, or years; or a quantity of people or objects. A double number strengthens its meaning. Numbers that stand alone usually do not refer to a time period. Instead, they carry a special connotation, such as the meanings related in this chapter.

Letters can highlight key events, objects, or the initials of important people in the inquirer's life. Double letters show that karma, cosmic forces, or circumstances beyond the inquirer's control are at work behind the scenes.

Both numbers and letters have their own implications apart from what's mentioned above. You may interpret them in a cosmic way if they stand out as large or isolated in the cup, or if the inquirer does not recognize any personal association.

Numbers

0—The zero digit can stand for loss or emptiness. On the other hand, it can also mean unity, fulfillment, and completion, especially if you see it as a circle. It can also symbolize a woman if it looks like an oval, or the alphabet letter *O*, and thereby takes on the significance of an initial. How you interpret this symbol very much depends on the surrounding images and your intuition.

1—beginnings, independence, self-reliance, individuality, freedom, strength, change, initiative, leadership, strong powers of concentration, someone born under the zodiac sign Leo.

2—partnership, parenting, nurturing, domestic concerns, second chance, intense emotions, conflict, change of residence, person born under the zodiac sign Cancer.

3—joy, happy social engagement, romance, love, visits from friends and relatives, parenthood, neighbors, short journeys, self-expression, talents, communications, writing, learning a new skill, the near future, someone born under the zodiac signs Aries or Scorpio.

4—firm foundation, organization, material achievement, mind over matter, discipline, concentration, patience, endurance, health issues, real estate, work and service, construction, secure retirement, real estate, good news, someone born under the zodiac signs Gemini or Virgo.

5—change, adaptability, versatility, conflict, strife, freedom, new paths opening, letting go, legal matters, overseas travel, foreign affairs, protection, someone born under the zodiac sign Sagittarius.

6—beauty, harmony, romance, creativity, social occasions, domesticity, marriage, pets, responsibilities, health, justice, someone born under the zodiac signs Taurus or Libra.

7—good luck, hidden influences, wisdom, analysis, perfection, the occult, people in positions of authority, public image, matters needing to be dealt with quickly, religion, someone born under the zodiac sign Capricorn.

8—ambition, power, attainment, renewal, courage, money, finances, efficiency, originality, independence, unexpected events, sudden changes in circumstances, someone born under the zodiac sign Aquarius.

9—wishes coming true, spiritual assistance, intuition coming into play, romance, inspiration, illusions, bad judgment, addiction, fortunate foreign connections, favorable outcome of legal matters, someone born under the zodiac sign Pisces.

10—marriage, perseverance, acceptance, dominion.

11—change, a stressful time ahead, vision, inspiration, idealism.

12—hiatus, success, special gifts.

13—transformation, a demanding period.

17—occult forces at work, phenomenal good luck.

22—mastery, success, practical idealism, involvement in humanitarian and/or global pursuits.

Letters

A—beginnings, study, inspiration, communication, artistry, the mind.

B—birth, fertility, nurturing, silence, relationships.

C—positive change, creativity, energy, enthusiasm, illumination, balanced sexuality.

D—brilliance, higher consciousness, enlightenment, danger.

E—achievement, effort, movement in affairs, adjustment to a situation.

F—failure, financial gain, comfort, fertility.

G—balance, sacrifice, generosity.

H—balanced power, forces beyond the inquirer's control, completion of a task.

I—the ego, restrictions, powers of concentration, an accident.

J—reward from past effort, the passage of time.

K—creativity, positive change, energy, transformation, illumination, enthusiasm.

L—growth, renewal, love, intuition, moving with the flow of life.

M—highly significant when found in the teacup; marriage, money, movement in the inquirer's affairs, loyalty, fertility, harmony, friendship, memory, or someone who has the inquirer's best interests at heart.

N—need, constraint, bondage.

O—perfection, faithfulness, freedom, property, matters concerning the inquirer's ancestors. (See entries under **circle** and the digit **0**, chapters 17 and earlier in this chapter.)

P—harmony, happiness, joy, laughter, fellowship, winning.

Q—a question.

R—the right path, good decisions, musical talent, ability to listen.

S—warmth, affection, motivation, inner light. If you are reading for a man, he will meet a strikingly beautiful woman. If you are reading for a woman, with care, she will become more beautiful than she ever imagined.

T—power, truth, self-sacrifice, victory, a plan being hatched.

U—courage, determination, persistence, ability to meet a challenge successfully.

V—sex appeal, victory.

W—laughter, joy, fellowship, well-being, winning, perfection, watchfulness.

X—change, enlightenment, crossed paths.

Y—uncertainty, a choice offered of two paths to follow.

Z—destruction, the end of a relationship or a project; alternatively, spiritual protection, connection with higher consciousness.

twenty-one

People and Human-Like Forms

In addition to the meanings listed here, a woman can be represented by a stick "wearing" a skirt or a frilly hat. A long stick or man's hat can symbolize a man, and a short stick, a child. As you learned in the last chapter, a letter may also refer to a person's name, as can a body part, or an article of clothing with which the inquirer associates the person. For example, a friend may be shown as a helping hand, and a teacher may be identified as a mortarboard (or, for that matter, an apple or a chalkboard). Following are more meanings.

Acrobat—the ups and downs of life, success after surmounting difficulties. The inquirer is juggling a dicey situation or handling too much.

Angel—love, happiness, peace, good news, spiritual advice. The inquirer is protected and providentially provided for.

Army—a stirring mass event.

Baby—persistent, small worries; a new project; an actual baby.

Chessman—concentration required now.

Child—promising future, period of apprenticeship, innocence, an actual child.

Clown—deception, mockery.

Crowd—gossip, a party.

Dancer—wish fulfilled, joy, celebration, attendance at a cultural event. The image may refer to an actual dancer.

Devil—temptation, too much emphasis on the material world.

Diver—The current situation requires deep thought or a thorough investigation. A diver may signify an actual diver or a trip by water.

Fairy—a rare sign meaning enchantment, joy, and unusually good fortune.

Farmer—renewal. Hard physical labor reaps rewards.

Ghost—Someone from the past is looking for the inquirer.

Giant—a father figure. (A mother figure may be represented by a container.)

Gnome—hidden treasure.

Hunter—swift action.

Jockey—speculation, love for a gambler.

Juggler—sales and marketing skills, multiple talents; may warn that the inquirer is juggling too many things.

Knight—message, a lover, mastery over a trade or a situation.

Man—a man, an authority figure, person born under the zodiac sign Aquarius.

Mermaid—temptation; an enchanting sea journey or beguiling prospect arriving from overseas.

Monk—desire to retreat from the world to contemplate life, spirituality, success through prayer.

Monster—terror, dark forces at work.

Nun—quarantine, discretion advised. If the inquirer is a woman, she may harbor a strong desire to leave behind the cares and woes of the world to pursue higher learning and a spiritual path.

Old Man or Woman—responsibilities.

Pedestrian—a message.

Person—an individual who will impact the inquirer's life or the actual inquirer, depending on the surrounding symbols. A human figure kneeling symbolizes prayer for guidance. If the figure is extending a hand, then someone will offer the inquirer help.

Policeman—help, protection, the law, someone in authority.

Profile—The traditional meaning is new friends, but I find that profiles occur often in cups and merely refer to people influencing the inquirer's life.

Rider—hasty, sudden news. (See also the **knight** entry earlier in this chapter.)

Skeleton—illness, poverty (See this and the skull entry in chapter 12 as well.)

Twins—events unfolding in groups of two, conflict, actual twins, person born under the zodiac sign Gemini.

Woman—a woman, a maternal figure, person born under the zodiac sign Virgo.

twenty-two

Plants

Since plants are living, growing things, in tea leaf reading they are almost always associated with abundance, fertility, prosperity, and wealth. Fruit represent earthly desires and fulfillment. Flowers and trees are so fraught with symbolism that I treat them in separate chapters.

> **Acorn**—success; progress, savings, good investments. Everything turns out better than hoped. When this symbol is found near the middle of the side of the cup, the inquirer

can expect better health. When it is near the top, financial success is on the way. Acorns also stand for virility, fertility, and the male sex organ.

Apple—thirst for knowledge, gain through education or business, long life, fulfillment, achievement of a goal, temptation. (See also chapters 16 and 21.)

Banana—good luck, happiness.

Beans—financial distress.

Cabbage—a sweetheart, jealousy, missed opportunities.

Cactus—stoicism, courage.

Carrot—opportunity, windfall.

Cherries—happy love affair, sensuality, good fortune. (See also chapter 16.)

Four-Leaf Clover—fantastic luck, prosperity, the nation of Ireland. The inquirer may have more than one lover.

Corn—fertility, harvest, the Midwest, the nation of Mexico.

Grapes—happiness, fulfillment, relaxation, romance, fertility, a party.

Grass—advice to move on.

Ivy—deep friendship, especially between women. An old house reveals its secrets.

Lemon—purity, a grudge, a sour situation.

Melon—good news, material gain.

Mushroom—expansion. If the image is found near the handle, the inquirer may make a new home abroad or in a forest. Mushrooms also symbolize the bounty of the earth; alternatively, a situation that has ranged out of control.

Orange—fertility, the state of Florida.

Pear—comfort, good fortune, a wealthy spouse or partner.

Pineapple—happiness, reconciliation, wealth, good health, a wish that comes true, a trip to Hawaii or to the beach.

Rosemary—situation or person worth remembering, somebody named Rosemary.

Strawberry—marriage proposal; personal finances improve. A magical time is in store for the inquirer where events will take on mystical significance.

Thistle—a Scot, a trip to Scotland. If your intuition tells you that the image represents a human being, the person is a tough survivor.

Vine—creativity, a protected location. Detective work is required to dig out information to benefit the inquirer.

Universal Symbols

It is not within the scope of this book to provide a complete compendium of universal symbols; only a sampling is related here. Perhaps the following short list will whet your appetite to do further research in a symbols dictionary or online. Most are drawn from ancient religions, including those of the ancient Egyptians, Muslims, Christians, Jews, and Pagans. You can find meanings for similar symbols in other chapters of Part Two, especially in chapter 17 on geometric shapes.

Ankh—a combination of a cross and the hieroglyph *ru,* meaning "mouth," "gateway," and "creative power." The ankh demonstrates dominion of spirit over matter. It grants life, love, power, and knowledge.

Buckle of Isis—known as *tjet,* it represents the blood of Isis, and confers her strength, goodwill and protection. The buckle is said to unlock hidden recesses and reveal secrets.

Caduceus—The intertwined snakes are often confused with the Rod of Asclepius, which is composed of one snake coiling around a staff and stands for the healing aspect of Mercury. The caduceus, when interpreted correctly, highlights another Mercurial aspect: commerce, theft, deception, and even death. However, many people, including most American health organizations and the US Army Medical Corps, have long taken this symbol as an emblem of healing, medicine, doctors, and healers. So whether you see one snake entwined or two, the meaning (as far as tea leaf reading is concerned), unless coupled with negative symbols, refers to healing.

Chain—an engagement or wedding, unity, constrictions.

Cornucopia—fruitfulness, prosperity, abundance.

Crescent—love with an exotic stranger or in a foreign location, a crossroads in life, the Middle East.

Cross—protection. A choice of two paths is offered. The inquirer's decision may have momentous implications, depending on surrounding symbols.

Hexagram—a six-sided star, it stands for protection, triumph of spirit over matter, and the truth; as well as the nation of Israel. (See also the **hexagram** entry in chapter 17.)

Ouroboros—cycle of eternal life.

Pentagram—protection, balance of mental and physical efforts, white Witchcraft. Depending on your spiritual orientation, you may interpret this symbol as a star. (See also the entries under **star** and **pentagon**, chapters 19 and 17.)

Scarab—the cycle of life, death, and rebirth. Hard work leads to success.

Shen—This Egyptian symbol of a circle resting on a horizontal line represents eternity and the bounty and power of the sun god.

twenty-four

Tools

The appearance of a tool in a cup may refer to a trade or occupation, such as a computer for a programmer or a spoon for a chef. A weapon indicates that the inquirer may be beset by enemies, and danger is imminent. Then again, this symbol may merely describe someone in the military, where arms are part of the job. If the tool resembles a piece of machinery, it may allude to the inquirer's work, but may also indicate the person's state of health, as in the "machinery of the body." Sporting goods are not listed here because there are so many of them. If you distinguish something like a tennis racket, or a hockey stick and the like, it may stand for one of the inquirer's interests or show movement in a situation.

Anchor—success, security, travel for the good of all concerned. At the **rim** of the cup, an anchor is interpreted as success through a lover or financial endeavor. If it appears in the **middle**, it foretells a successful voyage. An anchor at the **bottom** of the cup indicates that a social occasion will be pleasant and profitable.

Arrow—a message, virility, bad news, victory in accordance with divine law, plots, gossip, a secret romance. If **coupled with dots**, an arrow bodes distressing financial news. It may also point to another symbol, thereby stressing its significance.

Axe—troubles, difficulties overcome. The inquirer needs to make significant life changes.

Bow and Arrow—scandal, slander, jealousy, the zodiac sign Sagittarius.

Cane—period of ill health, advice to rest up. A cane may indicate an elderly person for whom the inquirer is responsible.

Compass—travel, change of job, new direction, fresh start.

Dagger—danger, a tense situation, jealousy, machinations of enemies, impetuousness.

Gallows—poor judgment.

Gavel—dealing with the law, courts, judges, attorneys, a judgment, finality.

Gun—an argument, violence. Pay close attention to the sign's placement in the cup to ascertain the location of the brutal act. If it is **close to the handle**, it may point to hostility in the home. If it is **opposite the handle**, then the incident may occur in a remote location.

Hammer—triumph over adversity, ruthlessness. Hard work leads to success. Headaches in the workplace require strong action. The inquirer is protected by the all-powerful god Thor. Alternatively, a hammer may refer to creativity with one's hands, for example, a sculptor.

Hoe—Hard work leads to success.

Key—a mystery, change of residence, questions answered. The inquirer will overcome current troubles. **Double** keys stand for a theft. **Crossed** keys represent honor, romance, and power.

Knife—the shadow self, quarrels, separation with ill feeling, vengeance. If **near the handle**, a knife may harbinger a divorce. If elongated into a **sword**, the meaning changes to triumph of the spirit over adversity. Someone may spread gossip about the inquirer. A knife may also refer to a surgical procedure.

Ladder—advancement through hard work, success, promotion, improving conditions. If **combined with love signs**, it may reveal an elopement.

Nail—injustice, maliciousness, a sharp pain, sudden illness, an architect.

Needle—trouble. A **needle and thread** show that a wish will be granted or that the inquirer will receive recognition for achievements.

Oar—time of increased activity. Help arrives during a difficult time.

Pendulum—uncertainty. It's time to move in a different direction.

Rake—need to clear up old business, a period of hard work ahead. **Coupled with other negative signs**, it means old grievances will return to haunt the inquirer.

Saw—outside interference, bad neighbors.

Scales—justice, legal matters, the zodiac sign Libra.

Scissors—a misunderstanding, separation; when **near the handle**, domestic strife. This ambivalent symbol represents birth and death, creation and destruction.

Spade—success harvested from hard work.

Transportation

Travel symbols often mean that the inquirer's affairs are on the move. Check to see if the symbol is pointed toward the handle or away from it. If looking toward the handle, it may indicate a visitor or an incoming influence. If pointed away, an influence is departing the inquirer's life or the inquirer will take a trip. Like machines, vehicles can symbolize the body and its state of health. They may also refer to a profession or an avocation, such as a boat for a fisherman or a car for a traveling salesman.

Airplane—travel, property, inheritance, promotion, a risky journey or sudden trip, success after trials and tribulations. When **pointing toward the handle**, an airplane signifies a visitation.

Ark—The inquirer will be provided for or saved from a natural disaster.

Bicycle—the circulatory system, the heart, sense of balance in life.

Boat—a message or visitation, refuge from trouble, happiness, recommendation to work harder to achieve goals, an educational journey.

Bus—The inquirer may be on the brink of taking an important journey with like-minded people, or to a location to meet and interact with a group.

Car—good luck, change in surroundings, travel close to home.

Cart—prosperity in business, a delay (as in "putting the cart before the horse").

Train—obsession, as in a "one-track mind"; being railroaded into doing something against one's will. The inquirer may feel stuck in routine and seek a way to break from the humdrum of quotidian existence.

Truck—career, a paternal figure.

Van—change of residence, business travel with coworkers, arrival of an important package.

Wagon—travel; a rough journey, either on the physical or mental plane; money troubles. Alternatively, a wagon may announce a wedding or a person with a pioneering spirit.

Trees

In general, trees stand for wish fulfillment, change for the better, endurance, good health, and family matters. It can tax your intuitive mind to identify a specific genus of tree inside a little teacup. As happens with flowers, if you manage to discern a certain type of tree, you will find that it holds a special meaning as follows:

> **Alder**—healing, alert to a health problem.
>
> **Almond**—purity, virginity, diplomacy. A
> blessed event will occur in the springtime.

Apple—love, fertility, fruition, temptation, esoteric knowledge, a school teacher. An apple may also refer to Glastonbury, England, thought to be the original "Isle of Apples" (Avalon). (See also chapters 16, 21, and 22.)

Ash—renewal, security, endurance.

Aspen—dealings with the elderly.

Bamboo—good luck and prosperity. A bamboo tree may refer to the Far East.

Bay—victory, success in sports, inspiration in creative pursuits.

Beech—education, messages, knowledge.

Birch—fertility, pregnancy, communication, discipline, the region of Scandinavia.

Branch—if **bare**, disappointment; if **leafed**, a birth; counsel to branch out and exercise compassion.

Bush—new friends, an invitation.

Cedar—longevity, prosperity, sacrifice.

Cherry—sweetness, secondary education, a young girl. (See also chapters 16 and 22)

Cypress—something sacred, a funeral, renewal, learning from past experiences.

Elder—communication or influence from the spirit world.

Elm—dignity.

Fig—fertility, protection, patience.

Fir—success in the arts, protection, child care.

Forest—unconscious fears, caution to think clearly and embrace the big picture. Many demands are being made on the inquirer. Alternatively, to see a forest may indicate that life will take an upturn, or that the inquirer will find a place of refuge from life's storms. The interpretation depends on the surrounding signs.

Hawthorn—a powerful ally, love, marriage; advice to tackle spring cleaning.

Hazel—a telepathic bond between two people. The inquirer may need to give an admirer the boot.

Juniper—protection, dealings with a Native American person.

Leaf—good news, fulfillment of ambitions. Leaves in a **cluster** mean happiness. The kind of tree the leaf is from also holds important symbolic value. For example, a **maple leaf** may stand for the nation of Canada, or a Canadian person.

Mistletoe—romance, sexuality, advice to seek a solution to a problem through candlelight meditation.

Oak—The tree, leaf, and **acorn** all mean strength, long life, vitality, prosperity, and bravery. A new direction is taken. The inquirer is favored by the gods.

Olive—peace, purity, good health; Mediterranean nations of Spain, Portugal, Italy, and Greece.

Palm—trip to a faraway tropical land, money, the good life, victory, fertility, abundance, the *anima,* success and honors.

Pine Tree or **Cone**—strength, vigor, prosperity, protection, immortality.

Rowan—knowledge, poetic inspiration, reminder to trust one's intuition.

Willow—delusions; sorrow, especially over family matters; femininity; grace. Lunar influences prevail.

Wood/Log, also a **Log Cabin**—cozy family life, happy marriage, desire to get away from the rat race.

Yew—visit to a churchyard.

Zodiac Symbols

Most people, even when their understanding of the divination arts is fuzzy, will at least know their astrological birth sign. Many check out their daily horoscopes in newspapers or online for guidance or entertainment. When you see zodiac signs or their related symbols in your teacup readings and you communicate their significance to your inquirers, you connect with them on a level which is already familiar and easy to comprehend.

Not a professional astrologer? Not to worry! You don't have to become an expert at recognizing these symbols and interpreting them. Luckily, the leaves have a way of arranging themselves in patterns you will be able to discern.

For those who would like a brief introduction to the significance of the signs of the zodiac, I offer some meanings in this chapter. Since the subject of the planets and asteroids is vast and reaches beyond the scope of this book, I give a keyword below to help your interpretation. To further expand your knowledge, I suggest you consult a good book on astrology, like *Larousse Encyclopedia of Astrology* (Jean-Louis Brau, Helen Weaver, and Allan Edmands. McGraw-Hill, 1983).

A zodiac sign seen in a cup can refer to many things, including a person born during that month, something that will happen at that time of year, or an attribution of the sign like a health issue or an occupation associated with it. Check coupled and surrounding images to make an accurate interpretation. The same goes for symbols of planets and the asteroids Ceres, Pallas, Juno, and Vesta.

The traditional planets and asteroids and their symbolic meanings are:

Ceres	⚳	fruition
Earth	⊕	materiality
Juno	⚵	beauty
Jupiter	♃	expansion

Mars	♂	action
Mercury	☿	adaptability
Moon	☽	intuition
Neptune	♆	the subconscious mind
Pallas	⚴	wisdom
Pluto	♇	transformation
Saturn	♄	responsibility
Sun	☉	vitality
Uranus	♅	invention
Venus	♀	relationships
Vesta	⚶	home

Signs of the Zodiac

Following are the signs of the zodiac and brief meanings as to character, career, and health.

♈ Aries (March 21–April 20)

Natives of this sign are active initiators who possess a pioneer spirit of adventure. They are at their best when roused by a challenge. Alert, observant, responsive, and courageous, they make excellent leaders, capable of executing unerring split-second decisions. They possess tremendous mental and physical energies, quick wits, and quicker tempers. Count on them to be enthusiastic, industrious, persistent, constructive, generous planners with bold ideas. Aries natives have been known to make great sacrifices in the name of justice and the principles of scientific thought.

When ill-aspected, Aries can become intemperate, lascivious, belligerent, impatient, irritable, selfish, jealous, disrespectful, excitable, and foolhardy. These people tend to live from crisis to crisis and will instigate one if need be. For better or worse, they rarely reflect on their mistakes and seldom follow through on the projects they initiate.

They do well at firefighting; police work; the steel, iron, and construction industries; sports; and writing and speaking. They make excellent surgeons, work well with medical equipment, and may become directors, managers, and instructors. The military is a compatible Aries career as long as the native is not required to follow too many strict orders.

Aries natives are blessed with strong bodies, abundant physical energy, good circulation, and sharp eyesight. They may suffer from sudden illnesses, headaches, cerebral congestion, nosebleeds, vertigo, encephalitis, smallpox, breakouts on the head and face, acne, ringworm, or sterility. Although strong, Aries natives tire easily when they worry and their general health may suffer. They require much rest, sleep, and peaceful surroundings to recuperate. This native should consume more vegetables and go easy on meat when under stress.

♉ *Taurus (April 21–May 20)*

Taurus solidifies the aggressiveness and verve of Aries into a determined, persistent, stable, and cautious individual. This sensitive native never forgets a grudge and patiently waits for the day when the tables are turned.

Those born under this sign may appear shy and retiring, but they store great amounts of latent energy and are capable of almost superhuman feats of endurance. Taurus is perfectly able to carry through on any project. They are also practical and conservative, and are often considered stodgy, especially by the natives of the more airy signs. Their apparent conservatism is born of true, deep-seated beliefs.

Taureans make solid advisors on money matters and are scrupulously honest. Their excellent physiques and innate sense of equilibrium make them consummate dancers and acrobats. They can be successful as art dealers, healers, mediums, public servants, officials, and executives. Many are drawn to art, music, literature, and forms of amusement.

Due to Venus' mitigating influence, these natives are generally pleasant, gentle, and sympathetic. When provoked, they can strike out in a headstrong and seemingly irrational manner. Yet they are responsible, cheerful, kind, loving people, fond of their homes and children.

Although rarely ill, when a native of this sign does succumb to an illness, recuperation is long and hard to achieve. Taurus is likely to have problems with the neck, chest, ears, thyroid gland, heart, bladder, and reproductive system. There is also the possibility of rheumatism, hemorrhoids, and trouble with the tonsils, palate, esophagus, uvula, and vocal chords.

♊ *Gemini (May 21–June 20)*

The person born under this sign is intelligent, quick, communicative, and sociable. These natives are keen observers of human nature, always seeking to understand the reasons for actions. They may be misconstrued as lacking heart by those who mistake their interest as a signal of commitment, since they tend to take mostly intellectual interest in others' problems.

Early in life, Gemini's naturally curious and dexterous mind needs to be channeled properly, or else out of boredom, the native may turn to deleterious activities. Gemini is best when asked to perform a variety of mentally stimulating tasks. Since Gemini is agile and adaptable, this person will either adjust to incompatible surroundings or change the environment to meet immediate needs. All in all, Gemini is a studious, skillful, intelligent, witty, versatile, and eloquent individual, around whom life is never dull.

When poorly aspected, Gemini tends to exhibit superficial knowledge, talk too much, engage in shallow relationships with others, lack firm opinions and ideals, show poor discrimination capabilities, and sometimes be a bit of a flake. Some Geminis are not to be trusted with money and may attempt to acquire it by scheming. This person may also be thought of as cold, childish, impressionable, or amoral.

Careers most suitable to natives of this sign include communications, teaching, music, art or literary critic, acting, advertising, sales, merchandising, printing, clerical work, reporting, jobs that change frequently or entail short journeys, and work which demands manual dexterity or constant use of their reasoning faculties.

Natives of this sign have generally good health. Even though they are not robust, disease has a hard time gaining a foothold in the bodies of these two-halves-that-make-a-whole. On the downside, they are highly nervous people who need regular periods of rest and above-average amounts of sleep in order to regroup their forces. They tend to suffer from hay fever and other allergies, colds, pinched nerves, sciatica, asthma, bronchitis, pleurisy, lung disease, and pneumonia. When they feel physically unbalanced, they should remember to eat energy-giving and nerve-balancing foods, cereals, and an overall bland diet.

♋ Cancer (June 21–July 22)

The natives of this sign are often quiet, reserved, sensitive, domestic, maternal, and protective. They have a knack for making money; generally they prosper and attract the limelight in spite of their shyness. When among friends, Cancers are quite sociable characters. They may show a great deal of devotedness and sympathy toward others, versatility, adaptability, and patience in unusual situations. They are receptive; industrious; given to exotic, adventurous experiences; and extremely susceptible to their surroundings.

On the downside, Cancerians can become possessive, sentimental, touchy, arrogant, xenophobic, resentful, disorderly, overly imaginative, inconsistent, grasping, untruthful, and indolent. They can be moody as well, and what would a crab be if it didn't occasionally snap at people?

They make assiduous seasonal workers, chemists, farmers, food processors, restaurateurs, advertisers, salespeople, and mediums. They work happily in the home, with children, and in health and social services. The hotel industry or any job that deals in sea products also attracts them. Cancers can become well-known public figures, achieving fame through their personal qualities. Several famous rock stars have been born under this sign. Moreover, this native possesses a flair for drama and is an impeccable gourmand.

Those born under this sign possess great emotional strength, but often let their bodies grow flabby. They need to learn to balance the fluids in their systems and focus their energies. They should avoid chills, the flu, and stomach disorders, all of which sap their strength. Cancers are susceptible to cancer, whooping cough, gastritis, and digestive ailments. They tend to be hypochondriacs.

A final word about this sign: Cancers make excellent psychics and musicians because they intuitively understand the world in a way which may not be apparent to others. They strike deep universal emotional chords in all human beings. This is one reason they can become trendsetters, not to mention consummate tea leaf readers.

♌ Leo (July 23–August 22)

Leos are fiery individuals who possess great strength of spirit and enjoy heroic action. The Leo native is a born leader. Those born under the sign of the lion have fine, noble, and generous natures, which contribute to making them idealistic, chivalrous, philanthropic, industrious, persistent, loyal, and ambitious. Here is an individual with an active mind, pleasant, affectionate disposition; powerful character, and more than a touch of flamboyance.

If negatively aspected, Leo can tend toward hotheaded, domineering behavior, especially in the family.

Leos can also become pompous, careless, bossy, and condescending.

Menial tasks and impersonal jobs do not appeal as much to Leos as those careers where they are free to take advantage of their considerable natural charisma. They often choose to become models, actors, dramatists, entertainers, executives, salespeople, or sports professionals.

Leo natives tend to suffer from the heat, over-exertion, eye problems, back strain, heart palpitations, careless accidents, spinal meningitis, fevers, aneurisms, and angina. Harmony in the home and moderation in all activities should be cultivated to mitigate these tendencies. Leo should consume high-energy foods, blood purifiers, and plenty of fluids.

♍ Virgo (August 23–September 22)

As the sixth sign of the zodiac, Virgo is associated with the astrological house of health, service, and work. Those born under the sign of the virgin tend to be neat, methodical, discriminating, prudent, and industrious. They show a love for detailed work, exceptional self-discipline, honesty, and an independent lifestyle. Virgo's motto is "I analyze."

These people can be overly cautious, hypercritical, too concerned about health, and hard taskmasters for themselves and others. This last characteristic emanates from Virgo's feeling that people are extensions of themselves. It is expected that others will measure up to Virgo's own high standards, and this native is disappointed when they do not. This especially applies to their love relationships. Although Virgos are tidy perfectionists, their closets and drawers are usually a mess. It is said that Virgo's mission in life is to learn to balance the spiritual and material worlds.

As for careers, Virgos shine in service jobs, teaching, writing, communications, mathematics, physics, biology, nursing, the arts, music, physical therapy, administrative work, and home-based activities. Nevertheless, they are jacks (or jills)-of-all-trades and do well in just about any chosen career.

In matters of health, these great analyzers are susceptible to bowel disorders, such as those diseases which affect the colon, intestines, and appendix. They may also suffer from nervous disorders. On the positive side, Virgos are renowned for their personal hygiene and physical attractiveness. More beautiful actresses are born under this sign than any other.

♎ Libra (September 23–October 22)

The native of this sign is a thoughtful, modest individual of great diplomacy, adaptability, and logical mind. Libra rules the seventh astrological house of marriage and partnerships. These people tend to engage often with friends and partners. They also involve themselves in contracts and legal disputes, usually appealing to reason in these matters.

Above all, friendly, cheerful Libras desire peace, harmony, and justice. They also adore refined pleasures, the arts, and music. They are tactful, cultured, persuasive, sympathetic, impartial, conciliatory, gracious, and idealistic, and they make happy mates.

When poorly aspected, they reveal weakness of will, indecisiveness, pedantry, vanity, recklessness, susceptibility, carelessness, impressionability, and aloofness.

Libras make estimable counselors, justices, clerks, bailiffs, social workers, mathematicians, accountants, bookkeepers, and lawyers. They dislike dirty work and are attracted to anything aesthetically pleasing. They make adept beauticians, designers, interior decorators, hosts for social functions, and dealers in apparel.

Their strength and energy are average. They are particularly susceptible to emotional strain, and in fact, the smooth, polished Libra façade often masks a good deal of edgy energy. This problem, along with depression, can be alleviated by active participation in sports. For kidney trouble, Libras should drink plenty of liquids and avoid extremes of heat and cold. They need to take care not to fall prey to nephritis, neuralgia, suppressing the need to urinate, lower back trouble, and ovarian cysts.

♏ *Scorpio (October 23–November 21)*

Scorpios exhibit the plutonian qualities of resourcefulness and dramatic intensity. Often the natives of this sign seem cool and reserved. It seems impossible to penetrate their icy façade, yet indefatigable energy and intense emotions roil beneath the tranquil surface. This endows them with immense power and the capacity for transcendence. Their passion makes them superb lovers.

On the negative side, Scorpios can be jealous, venomous, reclusive, secretive, and cruel, and they tend to nurture anger. Like the scorpion for which they are named, their stinging criticisms usually drive to the heart of the matter.

Their passionate interests may lead them to find careers where they are free to explore the ultimate mysteries of life and death. They may choose to become chemists, physicists, occultists, psychic healers, mediums, detectives, surgeons, dentists, astronomers, oceanographers, historians, politicians, or hypnotists.

Although blessed with a strong, muscular, vital constitution with excellent recuperative powers, this native needs to take care of the reproductive organs and the bladder.

In all, Scorpio is undoubtedly the most mysterious and profound sign of the zodiac. These natives make fascinating mates, friends, companions, and fellow workers.

♐ Sagittarius (November 22–December 21)

These intelligent natives love sports, dancing, and life in the open air. They also adore long-distance travel. For the Sagittarian, variety is the spice of life, and these people suffer when forced to follow boring schedules. When positively aspected, these people are enterprising, frank, self-reliant, sociable, cheerful, flexible, generous, loyal, and honorable. Sagittarians have a strong will to survive and a deep interest in philosophy.

When poorly aspected, these natives tend toward boisterousness, defiance, and rashness. Sagittarius people may become aggressive when aroused and may even turn prodigal.

Sagittarians make superlative writers, publishers, clerics, lawyers, judges, philosophers, interpreters, diplomats, travel agents, and teachers. Because Sagittarius is adept in so many areas, these people have a hard time deciding which career to pursue, and often end up with too many irons in the fire.

They rarely lack romance in their lives. However, their love relationships are inclined to be more platonic than passionate. They make generous lovers but may invoke jealousy, due to a wandering eye.

Since Sagittarius rules the liver and thighs, these areas should be cared for properly. A disposition toward overindulgence in alcohol must be curbed in order to maintain generally robust health and energy.

♑ *Capricorn (December 22–January 19)*

These are persevering people. When they meet with adversity—and they seem to encounter more obstacles than the natives of any other sign—they dig in their heels and endure until eventually they triumph. The native of this sign is extremely active, practical, businesslike, serious, ambitious, reliable, and diplomatic, of deep mind and good reasoning powers, and is a tireless worker. This patient individual has a stoic nature and self-denies life's luxuries. For Capricorn, the key to happiness is moderation in all things.

On the negative side, Capricorn, while receptive to people, is not necessarily open to other ideas, and perhaps relies too heavily on past experience for guidance. The natives of this sign, though conscientious, resent having to give more than their due. They also tend toward being authoritarian, overly materialistic, calculating, and shrewd. They may respect to a fault the accepted social norms and are scandalized by deviations in behavior.

In matters of career, the ambitious, hard-working Capricorn excels, and often achieves high honors and fame. These individuals make outstanding managers and organizers, political figures, historians, geologists, geographers, architects, civil engineers, civil servants, and miners. They also have a knack for raising herbs.

Capricorn natives are active, productive, enduring individuals who make dependable and conscientious friends and mates. Both genders have quiet strength, dignified posture, and elegant beauty.

Capricorns are blessed with tough, agile bodies. They possess strong bones and teeth, but suffer from problems with joints, nerves, being underweight, and sometimes herpes. Typical Capricorns have wiry frames and thick, dark hair that grays early.

≈ *Aquarius (January 20–February 18)*

The native of this sign is sociable, independent, refined, generous, intelligent, dignified, and patient. The sign rules astrology's eleventh house of hopes, wishes, friends, social activities, and clubs or organizations. Aquarius has a knack for originality and individualistic thinking based on reason and scientific thought.

Aquarians are geared toward humanitarian endeavors. They hold fixed opinions, but are not prejudiced. Though they may try to convince others to accept their views, they accord freedom of choice to all. Although they enjoy finding out what makes people tick, they treat everyone equally and impartially. Aquarians are thoughtful observers of life with an intuitive but philosophic bent. This individual is sincere, honest, refined, determined, unobtrusive, steady, cooperative, and a truth seeker.

Unfortunately, feelings for others do not run deep, which can make them frustrating as lovers. Aquarians tend to scatter their mental energies and may become nervous and anxious. They often adopt non-conforming political views and can be gullible.

They make excellent political leaders (in the mold of Lincoln, another Aquarian), computer manual writers, engineers, aviators, scientists, astrologers, inventors, artists, musicians, and literati. They are at their best when self-employed or when working under contract. They especially enjoy machine design and repair, and are in their element when able to collect, distill, and disseminate information.

Aquarians live on nervous energy and suffer from poor circulation, falls, sprains, weak ankles, anemia, blood poisoning, nervous diseases, hay fever, heart trouble, and cramps. They should take extra care of their eyes, too. They need vitamins to tone the blood, plenty of fresh air, water, fruit, and vegetables, and should avoid stimulants and greasy food.

♓ Pisces (February 19–March 20)

Pisces individuals are often shy, trusting, sympathetic, industrious, logical, idealistic, romantic, and imaginative. They love mystery and intrigue and possess phenomenal powers of concentration. When well-aspected, this idealism, flexibility, and imagination can lead them to soar to great heights of inspiration. Pisceans make perfect mates and hosts; they love their homes, animals, and children.

When poorly aspected, the native can be gullible, careless, dreamy, and overly sensitive. They can be very opinionated and can tend to see things only in black and white. They tend toward self-pity and self-deprecation, and can even fall into drug and alcohol use as an escape.

Pisces excels at acting, mimicry, poetic and fiction writing, dancing, sailing, and politics. This native can become a great healer and mystic if energies are properly channeled. Pisces does well at religious vocations and charitable work. Although the native can develop strong psychic abilities, there is a tendency to let these talents take over mind and body.

Pisces does not possess a strong physical body, for all is concentrated in spirit. These natives need regular meals and should take care not to ingest too much liquid. They suffer from coughs, colds, flu, deformities of the feet and toes, bunions, gout, glandular malfunctions, lung and bowel trouble, and contagious diseases. They must watch hygiene, diet, and sanitation more than the average person.

Short History of Tea

Love and scandal are the best sweeteners of tea.

—HENRY FIELDING, NOVELIST,
LOVE IN SEVERAL MASQUES

European traders first encountered the aromatic tea leaf when they traveled to China and bartered for it with merchants from the Fujian Province. Those tea traders spoke the Amoy dialect and pronounced the word for tea, *cha*, as "tay." From there, various spellings of the word *tea* made their way into many European languages. In Mandarin and Cantonese, the word is pronounced "chah." As such, it has gone into several languages, including Portuguese, Hindi, Persian, Russian, Turkish, Arabic, Tibetan, Korean, and Japanese.

Tea originated in China, where, legend has it, five thousand years ago an emperor discovered its use as a beverage when some leaves fell into a pot of water he was boiling. In another story from India, Bodhidharma, an Indian prince and Buddhist saint, kept dozing off while meditating outdoors. As an act of contrition for his weakness, he cut off his eyelids and flung them to the ground. Miraculously, two tea bushes sprang from the spot where the eyelids fell. The fact that so many legends have developed around the origin of tea attests to the esteem in which it is held in different cultures.

The story of this drink, once called "the froth of liquid jade," is packed with political intrigue and romance. Tea has, in part, provoked revolts around world. A prime example is the American colonies, where the high tax imposed on tea by the British without American representation was so detested that it eventually culminated in the Boston Tea Party and, subsequently, the war for independence.

This innocent-looking bush with leathery, dark green leaves and delicate, white blossoms has lured otherwise law-abiding citizens of many countries to engage in smuggling and drug trafficking. For example, by the middle of the eighteenth century, the British demand for tea from China had skyrocketed, but the Chinese did not want any British goods offered in trade. The British solution was to exchange opium grown in Bengal for tea. The Chinese government was not amused, and destroyed a large shipment of the drug. By 1839, Britain and China were at war. The situation only abated when India and Sri Lanka began producing large quantities of tea, thereby decreasing the demand for tea exclusively from China.

On the positive side, tea led to major tax reform in England. Throughout history and even today, the tea industry employs a large workforce. Because it is prepared with boiled water, tea consumption has kept people around the world healthy. Otherwise, so anthropologists tell us, many would have sickened and died from drinking water contaminated with bacteria and other toxins. Ancient people who imbibed large amounts of tea with their mainly meat diet also were probably healthier because of the vitamins and antioxidants they consumed in tea.

Over the centuries many have profited from tea, including growers, traders, merchants, and restaurateurs who established tearooms. Great fortunes, both legitimate and illegitimate, were amassed from tea during the days of the Yankee clippers in the nineteenth century. The first swift American ship to arrive in England reclaimed two-thirds of its building costs in a single cargo load. For many years, competing companies staged races to see who could sail from China with a full load and land first in the ports of London or New York. Those merchants who could provide tea in a timely manner to eager consumers came out ahead. Tea still predominates as the beverage of choice in Asian cultures.

Although tea is consumed less in continental western Europe, it took hold in Ireland and the United Kingdom, as well as in many of the former British colonies. In the seventeenth century, Catharine of Braganza, a Portuguese queen who married King Charles II, introduced tea to England. The beverage quickly became the preferred non-alcoholic liquid refreshment of all classes of society, despite its high price. Tea was so well-liked that moralists of the day, assuming that anything so good must be evil, raged against tea for drugging and debasing working-class women. Tea's virtues soon became apparent when people realized that it kept laborers alert and cheerful, and even increased production on the job.

At first, tea was such a luxury that most working-class consumers could only afford to drink it once a day at best. Middle and upper-class housewives kept the precious commodity under lock and key in caddies. The demand was so great that unscrupulous dealers adulterated the leaves with substances like elder flowers, sheep dung, and something called "smouch," a concoction of ash tree leaves and some unmentionables boiled in huge copper or iron cauldrons. With British tax reform that lowered tea's price and its increasing availability, tea eventually became affordable for all. The beverage took a prominent seat at the British dining table where it remains steadfast today, despite coffee's inroads.

appendix b

Tea for What Ails You
and More

*Drinking a cup of tea daily will surely
starve the apothecary.*

—CHINESE PROVERB

When I was little, my grandfather used to tell me, "When you've got your health, you've got everything. When you don't, all is lost." Grandpa was an Old World sort of person, whose daily breakfast consisted of oatmeal, an orange, and a cup of tea. Processed food probably never passed his lips. He rarely fell ill, and when it came time for him to pass on, he went into the hospital one night, and by the next morning, was gone.

I was too young then to understand the wisdom of his words, but since that time I have come to appreciate them. Throughout my adult life as part of my commitment to staying healthy, I have tried to maintain good eating habits and encourage my family to do the same. This salubrious lifestyle includes drinking tea instead of coffee and soda.

Here's to Your Health!

Claims about tea's health benefits extend as far back as 2737 BCE to the Emperor Shen Nung of China. He is alleged to have said that tea provides "vigor of body, contentment of mind, and determination of purpose." Centuries later in 780 CE, Lu Yu, who wrote the first known book about tea, declared that the drink cured ills as far-ranging as headaches, depression, constipation, and sore muscles. Emperors' physicians who prescribed tea for common ailments must have set great stock by the leaves' curative powers, because as long as the head of state remained well, the doctor was maintained in luxury. Woe betide the physician if the emperor fell ill, for in that circumstance, the doctor lost his head!

The British incorporated "a nice cuppa" into their lifestyle and still drink it to cure ailments, especially those of emotional origin. So highly regarded is tea in the British Isles that the popular Typhoo brand is so named for the Chinese word for "doctor." The PG Tips brand initials stand for "pre-gestive," which underscores the belief that tea is good for digestion.

It seems that people from many cultures, including Americans, trust in the ability of tea—especially green tea—to help prevent disease and fortify the body.

Is There Anything Bad about Tea?

Studies relating to tea's health merits have shown how this drink can positively affect heart disease, aging bones, stress and anxiety, digestion, dental health, weight management, certain cancers, and even Alzheimer's. The popular press sometimes latches on to such reports and inflates the results for the consumption of readers eager for a miracle panacea.

The truth is, like many botanicals, tea's action is slow and it tends to work more on the whole body rather than aggressively attacking a specific ailment.

If you are a green tea drinker, you should be aware that certain medications interact with it negatively. If you take atropine, Cardec DM, codeine, ephedrine, pseudoephedrine, Lomotil, Lonox, theophylline, aminophyline, or warfarin, you should consult your physician or pharmacist before drinking green tea.

Tea contains caffeine, which can aggravate high blood pressure, overstimulate the heart, and cause breakouts in people with acne-prone skin. Also the ever-present tannins are strong enough to corrode metal. To get a balanced assessment, let's first tackle the caffeine issue.

Tea and Caffeine

Pound for pound, dried black tea contains twice the caffeine of coffee. However, you can brew approximately two hundred cups of tea from a pound—more, if you like your tea weak—as opposed to only around forty cups of coffee. The amount of caffeine depends on how much oxidation has occurred. According to the American Tea Council, green and white teas contain approximately 15 to 30 mg of caffeine per eight-ounce cup. The Council also notes that fully oxidized black teas weigh in at only 35 to 50 mg. Oolongs fall in a range somewhere between the green and black teas. Lipton, the most widely drunk brand in the United States, has been measured to contain 35 to 40 mg. In contrast, eight ounces of brewed coffee will provide you with a 135 to 140 mg jolt.

So, is the caffeine in tea really all that bad for you? I suppose the answer largely hinges on your individual body's health. If, for example, you have fibrocystic disease or high blood pressure, caffeine will only aggravate your condition. The amount of caffeine you consume also depends on how much tea you drink and how strong a brew you prefer.

Findings from the Linus Pauling Institute show that you shouldn't drink green tea if you have abnormally low serum potassium. However, you would have to drink between three and four liters per day for the tea to affect your serum potassium levels adversely—surely you would become water-logged before that occurred! If you ingest at least six grams of tea extracts per day, you may experience moderate gastrointestinal side effects like diarrhea and tremors. Extracts are strong concentrations of tea—too strong, in fact, to be enjoyed without diluting them. I think you would have to be a tea extract fanatic to consume enough to harm you.

You may also have caffeine sensitivity, like me. If I drink just a half cup of coffee, I soon become nervous, jittery, and exhausted, yet can't fall asleep for hours. By contrast, unless I've drunk at least ten cups of tea during the day, tea doesn't bother me at all. In fact, I often drink it as a nightcap. The reason I don't get wobbly drinking tea probably has to do with the muscle relaxants in it I will explain shortly.

Science has proven that the caffeine in tea activates the respiratory and central nervous systems as well as the kidneys. But tea also contains the mild muscle relaxants theophylline and theobromine. It seems you can relax but remain alert if you drink tea. Rather like having your cake and eating it, too.

Caffeine levels peak within an hour of entering the bloodstream, which is one reason some long distance runners and triathletes drink it before working out. The nineteenth-century English prime minister

William Gladstone, a great promoter of tea, was right on the mark when he claimed:

If thou art cold, tea will warm thee,
If thou art hot, tea will cool thee,
If thou art sad, tea will cheer thee,
If thou art cross, tea will calm thee.

Then there's the taste factor: caffeine interacts with tea's essential oils and its polyphenols, a class of tannins, to create a fragrantly seductive flavor.

If you are still uncomfortable with tea's caffeine content, consider sticking to herbal infusions, white or green tea, or drink it decaffeinated. If you go the decaffeinated route, be aware that some decaffeinated tea on the market is processed with ethyl acetate, a highly flammable solvent also used in nail polish (!). This solvent can irritate the skin and cause coughing, dizziness, headache, nausea, as well as a sore throat if inhaled. To be safe, you should look for manufacturers who decaffeinate their teas with carbon dioxide and water to eliminate potentially harmful chemicals. The more naturally tea is decaffeinated, the more antioxidants and flavor in the tea.

You can also do a second potting. Since caffeine dissolves in boiling water, tea steeped for as few as three minutes will lose approximately one-half of its caffeine. If you are concerned about caffeine, simply remove the leaves after steeping and transfer them to a second, empty pot. Pour boiling water over them and steep again. You will have reduced the amount of caffeine contained in the tea by approximately 50 percent.

Tea and Tannins

The tannins that give tea its unique taste are not the ones used to tan leather. Tea's tannins, like those in red wine, interact with proteins in the mouth to cause an astringent taste that functions as an antiseptic. This process helps the stomach digest fatty foods and fight alkaloid poisons and bacteria. Tannins are also a class of catechin, an anti-cancer antioxidant that cuts down on the damage done to lipids and DNA during digestion. In addition, tannins keep the body from absorbing cholesterol.

If you still object to tannins, try adding milk to your tea. You'll miss out on the antioxidants, but the tannins will bind to the milk's proteins rather than to yours, and will pass harmlessly through your body (unless you're lactose intolerant, of course).

The Essence of Tea

Certainly tea is every bit as good for you as water, the world's most popular beverage. It is thought that after tea's popularization in Britain, the very fact that the water had to be boiled in order to prepare it reduced incidences of infections and disease among all social classes. Another point in favor of tea is that unlike many other beverages, it contains no calories, phosphates, artificial sweeteners, or colors.

In addition to the caffeine, tannins, theophylline, and theobromine, the following are present in non-herbal tea:

Vitamins and Minerals
These include vitamins A, B complex, C, D, K, and traces of manganese and amino acids. Anthropologists posit that because some exclusively meat-eating ancient cultures of central Asia also drank a lot of tea, their bodies absorbed from it enough vitamins and minerals to stay reasonably healthy.

Antioxidants
Besides the tannins described above, tea includes twelve types of nutrients known as flavonoids. Catechins, a type of flavonoid, are considered to be more powerfully antioxidant than vitamins A, C, E, and beta carotene. Antioxidants bind free radicals—the oxygen-containing molecules in your body that result from the breaking down of food for energy. Free radicals can damage cells and tissues over time and contribute to chronic conditions like cancer and heart disease. A recent *Consumer Reports* analysis shows that drinking just one eight-ounce cup of green tea every

day can carry the same antioxidant potency as one cup of blueberries. Black teas possess similar properties.

Fluoride

Green and white teas contain more of this substance, while black has a lesser amount. The Japanese custom of consuming a cup of green tea after a meal both helps the digestion and inhibits growth of the bacteria that cause bad breath.

EGCG

Otherwise known as epigallocatechin 3-gallate, this flavonoid, present in green tea as well as in fruit and vegetables, is an antioxidant more powerful than vitamin E. It can control the activity of free radicals and keep them from damaging and destroying cells in our bodies. EGCG may also help boost the immune system, although more studies need to be done to substantiate this claim. For a long time, the British have known about EGCG, at least intuitively. As a culture, they prefer to take tea to prevent and treat colds and flu, rather than medicate themselves with pills, as do many Americans.

Tea Fights Disease

Research into tea's effects on health was initiated in the 1980s when interest in tea as a disease preventative began to increase. Initially, scientists worked to find out why some drinkers are less likely to develop certain diseases, and which of tea's components are relevant. From this research has emerged evidence that tea, especially green tea, can prevent and mitigate the effects of a variety of disorders. In fact, the University of Maryland Medical Center website (www.umm.edu/altmed/articles/green-tea-000255. htm) cites more than forty articles pointing to the power of green tea to ameliorate or prevent disorders as varied as coronary and liver disease; diabetes; inflammatory bowel syndrome; stomach, esophageal, pancreatic, prostate, colon, breast, and bladder cancers; Alzheimer's; and even tooth decay.

Here are a few tea recipes designed to address common health problems. If you have a specific ailment, I advise you to consult your doctor. Teas are meant to support your system, not to be taken as substitutes for traditional medicine. As with any botanical, make certain you are not allergic to any of the ingredients before you consume them.

Invincible Woman Tea

This is a superior tea for the reproductive system at any stage in a woman's life. Combine ½ cup Gunpowder Green tea, 1 tablespoon raspberry leaves, 1 teaspoon crushed rosehips, 1 teaspoon black cohosh root, 1 teaspoon dong quai root, ½ teaspoon parsley root, and ¼ teaspoon licorice powder. Use one teaspoonful per cup of boiling water.

Heart-Healthy Tea

Studies have proven that drinking one cup of green tea per day reduces by 38 percent the risk of atherosclerosis, a condition that can lead to coronary malfunction. The following recipe will help keep your heart pumping in tiptop condition. Combine 1 cup Gunpowder Green tea, ¼ cup crushed hawthorn berries, 1 tablespoon black cherry bark, and 2 teaspoons rosemary. If you wish, add a dash of capiscum (paprika). Use one teaspoonful per cup

Sunny Smiles Tea

Green tea is said to be good for strengthening teeth and bones. The catechins in green tea have been shown to strengthen teeth and gums and help prevent cavities and gum disease. The polyphenols also help prevent plaque from sticking to tooth enamel. As an added benefit, the fluoride and phytoestrogens also help guard against osteoporosis.

Combine 1 cup of any variety of green tea that strikes your fancy with 1 tablespoon maca root, 1 tablespoon echinacea root, 1 teaspoon bayberry root, and ½ teaspoon crushed cloves. Again, use one teaspoonful per cup

Brand New Day Tea

The following formula is guaranteed to bring a little sunshine to your morning, especially when it's cloudy. Drink it when you have stayed out way too late the night before and need to energize yourself for the day ahead. My recipe renders a large amount, so you can always have some ready when you need it. Use only one teaspoonful or less per cup.

Combine 1 cup English Breakfast or Ceylon tea with 1 tablespoon peppermint, 1 tablespoon nettles, 1 teaspoon guaraná, ½ teaspoon ginseng, and ¼ teaspoon ginger.

Silent Night Tea

As the last recipe helps wake you up, it is appropriate to include one to aid sleep. White tea has been proven to lower the blood pressure, so I use it as a key ingredient of this formula. The other reason I have chosen white tea is that it is truly one of my favorite varieties. If you find white tea to be too mild, you can always substitute a green tea like Dragon Well or Sencha.

Combine 1 cup Silver Needle or White Peony white tea with ¼ cup German chamomile, 1 tablespoon hops, 1 tablespoon lemon catmint, 1 tablespoon lemon balm, and ½ teaspoon valerian root. Use up to one teaspoonful per cup of boiling water. Happy dreams!

Considering the abundance of available data and delicious recipes, the next time you toast someone's health, you might consider doing it with a cup of tea instead of a glass of wine.

glossary

Afternoon Tea—Tea served approximately between three and five o'clock along with accompanying finger food. Sometimes called Low Tea.

Black Tea—Fully oxidized tea leaves, which are then fired or dried. Often they are used for complex or year-long tea leaf readings.

Brick Tea—Tea from China and Japan mixed with stalks and dust, molded into bricks under high pressure. In the past, this made a convenient form to transport tea overland by caravan.

Camellia sinensis, also ***Thea sinensis***—Flowering evergreen tree pruned to the size of a shrub, the source of all true tea.

Ceylon Tea—A fine-leaf black tea with a crisp citrus aroma, grown in Sri Lanka. In tea leaf reading, it often is used for detailed readings.

China Tea—A fine-leaf black tea that usually renders numerous images.

Chinese Gongfu—A Chinese way to prepare and serve tea, which, although elaborate, takes place in a more relaxed environment than the Japanese Tea Ceremony.

Constant Comment—This aromatic blend of black tea, orange rind, and sweet spice created by the Bigelow tea company makes an excellent choice in tea leaf reading for questions centered on family and relationships.

Cream Tea—Afternoon Tea served with tea, scones, jam, and Devonshire cream.

Darjeeling Tea—Known as the champagne of teas for its muscatel flavor, this tea is grown in the Darjeeling Hills of India.

Decoction—A medicinal brew of botanicals other than *Camellia sinensis.* The plant parts are boiled and simmered for ten to twenty minutes in order to release the essences from the roots, seeds and barks. Decoctions are far stronger than infusions, and usually are not at all pleasant-tasting.

Divination—The art of prognostication; that is, foretelling the future. The term sometimes also refers to character analysis. The diviner is able to tap into a subconscious source and become aware of past, present and future events, which are often received in symbolic form. A tea leaf reader is a diviner who is able to interpret the symbols left in a teacup after the tea is drunk.

English Breakfast Tea—A full-bodied, colorful blend of black teas that works well for general readings. Drink this tea in the morning to foresee events that will take place throughout your day.

Earl Grey Tea—This fine-leaf black tea scented with oil of bergamot often produces many detailed images in the teacup. Its peppery aroma is a favorite of many tea drinkers.

EGCG—Acronym for a flavonoid present in green tea that may help boost the immune system and keep free radicals from damaging and destroying the body on a cellular level.

Estate—A property, formerly known as a plantation, where tea is grown. It may include more than one garden where tea is produced under the aegis of one owner or manager.

Flavonoid—Also known as a bioflavonoid, it is a nutrient and antioxidant present in tea that is known to fight cancer and heart disease.

Full Tea—Afternoon tea served with sandwiches, scones, sweets, and dessert.

Geomancy—Divination practiced worldwide, where the diviner throws objects on the ground or a table, or draws dots at random on paper, and interprets the ensuing patterns. The systems used to decipher the patterns vary from simple (e.g., African bone divination) to complex (e.g., the I Ching). Tea leaf reading is a form of geomancy.

Green Tea—Tea leaves that are withered, steamed, or heated, then immediately rolled and dried. The appearance of the brewed tea and flavor are both light.

Gunpowder Tea—A coarse green tea rolled into pellets. After they dry, the leaves take on the grayish appearance of gunpowder. This tea usually produces only a few bold images in the cup, making it ideal for short or single-question tea leaf readings.

High Tea—An informal tea, often just for family members, taken at the higher dining room table, as opposed to the lower coffee-style table.

India Tea—Tea grown in the Indian provinces of Assam, Darjeeling, and Nilgiri. Approximately

14,000 tea estates exist in India today, and the industry employs over one million workers.

Infusion—Tea made by steeping botanicals in hot water. Beverage and medicinal infusions differ according to the length of time the botanicals are steeped. For a beverage tea, steep 3 to 5 minutes. For a medicinal infusion, simmer for 5 to 10 minutes, or until the liquid is reduced by one-third. Strain away the botanicals before drinking.

Inquirer—The person having a tea leaf reading; sometimes called the "querent" or "client."

Intuition—The ability to know or learn something immediately as a perception or insight, without having recourse to conscious reasoning. Almost everyone possesses this right-brain function to a greater or lesser extent. It can be developed and enhanced through practice as one would do to learn to play a musical instrument. Intuition plays an important role in tea leaf reading.

Japanese Tea Ceremony—An elegant and formal way of taking tea that uses a special powdered green tea called matcha.

Lapsang Souchong Tea—A fine leaf, smoked black tea originally from the Fujian province of China. Its heady aroma is reminiscent of an oak fire. In tea leaf reading, this tea can quite accurately predict answers to questions about travel, exotic places, and changes of residence.

Light Tea—Afternoon tea served with light refreshments such as scones and cakes.

Low Tea—Afternoon tea served at a low table like a coffee table. Polite conversation and musical entertainment often form an enjoyable part of the Low Tea or Afternoon Tea experience.

Matcha—Special powdered green tea drunk during the Japanese Tea Ceremony. Although it has a fine flavor as a beverage tea, its powdery consistency makes it unsuitable for tea leaf reading.

Maté—Also known as yerba maté, this infusion is made from the leaves of a native subtropical South American evergreen. By tradition, it is sipped through a silver straw from a hollowed-out gourd.

Meat Tea—Another name for High Tea. It is so called because heartier fare is served than what is offered for Afternoon Tea.

Ochazuke—Japanese tea soup often drunk after a heavy meal, at lunch, late at night, or as comfort food.

"One for the pot"—Refers to the English custom when preparing tea, to put one teaspoonful of dried leaves in the pot for each person present, then add one extra teaspoonful before pouring in the hot water.

Oolong Tea—Semi-oxidized tea leaves from China and Taiwan.

Psychic—As a noun, the term describes a person who is sensitive to paranormal occurrences, or who demonstrates a facility for paranormal abilities, such as telepathy, clairvoyance, precognition, and the ability to see auras. In tea leaf reading, it is useful to be somewhat psychic, but not necessary. A person's native intuition and ability to remember symbols play an equal and perhaps greater role in the interpretation of the leaves.

Quantum Physics—The branch of physics based on quantum theory, which posits that subjects are interrelated without any force acting on them or any communication between them. It is said that in this way tea leaves help connect the reader to the inquirer and to the inquirer's future.

Reader—The person who interprets the tea leaf patterns left in the cup after the tea is drunk. Also called the interpreter.

Red Tea *(Aspalathus linearis)*—Popular name for a red-colored tea that comes from the honey bush. It is also called Rooibos or Red Bush tea. The tea is green-colored until oxidized. This strong antioxidant is said to strengthen the capillary walls.

Scented Tea—Tea to which flower blossoms, fruits, spices, or essential oils have been added during production. Examples include Jasmine, Earl Grey, Cinnamon, and Rose Puchong.

Second Potting—A way to remove excess caffeine from tea. The leaves are removed after steeping, and transferred to a second empty pot. Boiling water is then poured over the leaves and they are steeped again.

"Shall I be mother?"—Refers to the British custom of one person who volunteers to take on the responsibility of serving the tea to family members and guests. Traditionally, this was the mother's duty in British households. Today anybody well versed in the niceties of serving tea can assume the role.

Symbol—In tea leaf reading, it is an image formed by the tea leaves that stands for, or represents something else. For example, a spider could represent industriousness, or a book might symbolize education or wisdom.

Tannins—Astringent polyphenol compounds similar to substances in red wine that interact with the proteins in the mouth to give tea its pungency and taste. Tannins are also present in coffee and many botanicals.

Tasseomancy—Also known as tasseography or tea leaf reading. It is the ancient Chinese art of interpreting the patterns left by tea leaves in the bottom of a teacup after the tea is drunk.

Tea and Food Pairing—Art of putting together food and teas to complement and enhance each other's flavors.

Tea Grades—See entries in the second section of this glossary.

Teahouse/Tearoom—Venues where tea and light accompaniments are served. They may also be called tea shops.

Tea Leaf Reading—Art of deciphering the patterns made by the tea leaves left over in a cup after the tea is drunk. The purpose is to discover the drinker's tendencies and environmental factors that are believed to influence the person's future.

Teetotaling—Pertaining to or advocating total abstinence from alcoholic drinks. "Tee" refers to the reduplication of the letter *T* and not, as is popularly supposed, to the habit of drinking tea in place of alcohol.

Thea sinensis also ***Camellia sinensis***—The flowering evergreen pruned to the size of **a shrub, from which all true tea originates.**

Tisane—Traditional name for a drinking infusion composed of botanicals not derived from the *Camellia sinensis* bush. Nowadays most people other than tea masters and purists refer to these infusions as herbal teas.

White Tea—Tea produced from the unopened buds and youngest leaves of the tea plant. White tea has a delicate flavor.

Zodiac Teas—Tea blends consisting of various teas and other botanicals believed to be associated with the signs of the zodiac. A reader may use a zodiac blend that pertains to the inquirer's birth sign in order to obtain a year-long reading.

Tea Grades

You don't need to memorize a lot of data about grades of tea to give a superior tea leaf reading, or to enjoy drinking a good cup of tea. Nevertheless, some of you may be curious about the meaning of all those capital letters you find on some packaging such as FOP, TGFOP, and BOP. Some may also appreciate further guidance than what you have already learned about how to select fine teas. Tea grades give you the answers to these questions. This section lists some of the more common tea grades and related terms and conveys brief descriptions. For in-depth resources on tea grades, please refer to the bibliography.

(P) **Pekoe**—A whole-leaf black tea that comes from plucking the second leaf on the tea bush. In Chinese, the term means "white hair" and refers to the white or yellow down found on the backs of the young tea leaf.

(OP) **Orange Pekoe**—A large-leaf black tea which has fewer tips than a Flowery Orange Pekoe. The grade is usually, although not always, better than Pekoe.

(FP) **Flowery Pekoe**—Flowery means that the whole, thin leaf of the black tea is rolled lengthwise.

(FOP) **Flowery Orange Pekoe**—Refers to either a whole-leaf or broken-leaf black tea with a lot of tip, which gives it a finer quality.

Tip/Tippy—Tea that has an abundance of tips; that is, the yellow or white hair on the youngest leaves.

(TGFOP) **Tippy Golden Flowery Orange Pekoe**—"Golden" refers to the light color of the buds. This is a high grade of full-leaf tea that usually comes from Darjeeling or Assam.

Broken Grades—Teas that are crushed mechanically.

(BOP) **Broken Orange Pekoe**—A black tea composed of broken segments of somewhat coarser leaves without tip. BOP makes a slightly finer tea than OP.

(FTGFOP1) **Fine Tippy Golden Flowery Orange Pekoe, Grade 1**—The most sought-after grade of tea. It is loaded with tips and young tea leaves. The common joke floating around the industry about this grade is that the initials stand for "Far Too Good For Ordinary People."

Souchong—This black tea grade refers to large, whole leaves curled at the edges and twisted lengthwise.

(CTC) **Crushed, Torn, and Curled**—Description of the method by which some leaves are processed. In the past, the two tiny leaves from the end of each branch were hand-picked. This is called the "orthodox method," and it is still done today in some very small, exclusive tea gardens. The CTC method uses machines that often snatch up the entire twig and branch, which later must be removed.

Choppy—Tea that contains leaves of various sizes. Not to be confused with "chop." The latter term, originating in India, refers to the stamp of a number, mark, or brand on the tea.

Fannings—Small, grainy leaf particles about the size of a pinhead that have been sifted from the better grades of tea. The liquor that comes from fannings sometimes is as good as that of whole-leaf grades.

Dust—These are the smallest particles of leaf size left over after the completion of the manufacturing process. Since they infuse quickly and have a full flavor and strength, they are often used for teabags. The quality of dust, however, is not as good as that of other grades.

bibliography

Books

Barker, Cicely Mary. *How to Host a Flower Fairy Tea Party*. London: The Penguin Group, 2004.

Bard, Sharon, Brigit Nielsen, and Clara Rosemarda. *Steeped in the World of Tea*. Northampton, MA: Interlink Books, 2005.

Barnes, Emilie. *An Invitation to Tea*. Eugene, OR: Harvest House Publishers, 2009.

Blofeld, John. *The Chinese Art of Tea*. Boston: Shambhala, 1985.

Dolby, Victoria, and Lester A. Mitscher. *The Green Tea Book: China's Fountain of Youth*. Garden City Park, NY: Avery Publishing Group, 1996.

Dunnewind, Stephanie. Illustrations by Capucine Mazille. *Come to Tea: Fun Tea Party Themes, Recipes, Crafts, Games, Etiquette and More*. New York: Sterling Publishing Company, Inc., 2002.

Farley, Helen. *The Complete Guide to Tea-leaf Reading*. Port Melbourne, Victoria, Australia: Thomas C. Lothian Pty. Ltd., 2000.

Fenton, Sasha. *Tea Cup Reading: A Quick and Easy Guide to Tasseography*. York Beach, ME: Weiser Books, 2000.

Fontana, Marjorie A. *Cup of Fortune: A Guide to Tea Leaf Reading*. Madison, WI: Fantastic, 1979.

Gautier, Lydia. *Tea*. San Francisco: Chronicle Books, 2006.

Gottlieb, Dawn Hylton, and Diane Sedo. Illustrations by Darlene Jones. *Taking Tea with Alice*. Perryville, KY: Benjamin Press, 2008.

Harney, Michael. *The Harney and Sons Guide to Tea*. Hong Kong: Penguin Press, 2008.

Harvest House Publishers' Authors. *365 Things Every Tea Lover Should Know*. Eugene, OR: Harvest House Publishers, 2008.

Heiss, Mary Lou, and Robert J. Heiss. *The Story of Tea: A Cultural History and Drinking Guide.* Berkeley, CA: Ten Speed Press, 2007.

Hepburn, Rae. *Tea Leaf Fortune Cards.* Boston: Journey Editions, 2000.

Hewitt, William W. *Tea Leaf Reading.* St. Paul: Llewellyn Publications, 1999.

Highland Seer. *Reading Tea-Leaves.* Introduction by James Norwood Pratt and afterword by John Harney. New York: Clarkson Potter Publishers, 1993.

Hohenegger, Beatrice. *Liquid Jade: The Story of Tea from East to West.* New York: St. Martin's Press, 2007.

Johnson, Dorothea and John Harney. *Children's Tea and Etiquette.* Perryville, KY: Benjamin Press, 2007.

Johnson, Dorothea, and Bruce Richardson. *Tea and Etiquette.* 2nd ed. Perryville, KY: Benjamin Press, 2009.

Kemp, Gillian. *The Fortune-Telling Book.* Boston: Little, Brown and Company, 2000.

MacFarlane, Alan, and Iris MacFarlane. *The Empire of Tea: The Remarkable History of the Plant That Took Over the World.* New York: The Overlook Press, Petyer Mayer Publishers, Inc., 2004.

Marcin, Marietta Marshall. *Herbal Tea Gardens: 22 Plants for Your Enjoyment and Well-Being.* Pownal, VT: Storey Books, 1999.

Martin, Laura C. *Tea: The Drink That Changed the World.* Hong Kong: Periplus Editions, Ltd., 2007.

Mellor, Isha. *The Little Tea Book.* Avon, England: Piatkus, 1985.

Morwyn. *The Complete Book of Psychic Arts.* St. Paul, MN: Llewellyn Publications, 2000.

———. *Green Magic: The Healing Power of Herbs, Talismans, and Stones.* West Chester, PA: Whitford Press/Schiffer Publishing, 1994.

Norman, Jill. *Teas and Tisanes.* New York: Bantam Books, 1989.

Okakura, Kakuzo. *The Book of Tea.* A free, downloadable e-book from Project Gutenberg.

Perry, Sara, and Alison Miksch. *The New Tea Book: A Guide to Black, Green, Herbal, and Chai Tea.* San Francisco: Chronicle Books, 2001.

Pettigrew, Jane. *Afternoon Tea.* Perryville, KY: Benjamin Press, 2008.

———. *The Tea Companion: A Connoisseur's Guide.* 2nd ed. Perryville, KY: Benjamin Press, 2009.

Pratt, James Norwood. *The Tea Lover's Treasury.* Introduction by M.F.K. Fisher. San Ramon, CA: 101 Productions, 1993.

Pruess, Joanna, and John Harney. *Eat Tea: Savory and Sweet Dishes Flavored with the World's Most Versatile Ingredient.* Guilford, CT: Globe Pequot Press, 2001.

Richardson, Bruce. *The Great Tea Rooms of America.* 4th ed. Perryville, KY: Benjamin Press, 2008.

———. *The Great Tea Rooms of Britain.* Perryville, KY: Benjamin Press, 2008.

Richardson, Lisa Boalt. *Tea with a Twist: Entertaining and Cooking with Tea.* Eugene, OR: Harvest Home Publishers, 2009.

Schafer, Charles, and Violet Schafer. *Teacraft: A Treasury of Romance, Rituals, and Recipes.* San Francisco: Yerba Buena Press, 1975.

Struthers, Jane. *The Art of Tea-Leaf Reading.* London: Godsfield Press, Octopus Publishing Group Ltd., 2006.

Ukra, Mark. *The Ultimate Tea Diet: Boost Your Metabolism, Shrink Your Appetite, and Kick-Start Remarkable Weight Loss.* New York: Harper Collins, 2008.

Waller, Kim. *The Art of Taking Tea.* New York: Sterling Publishing Company, Inc., 2005.

Wilson, Joyce. *How to Read Tea Leaves.* New York: Bantam, 1969.

Yi, Dang. *Chinese Health Tea.* Beijing: New World Press, 2007.

Magazines and Internet Resources

www.houdeasianart.com. *The Art of Tea.* A monthly since 2007 that focuses on Chinese tea.

www.freshcup.com. *Fresh Cup Magazine.* For tea and coffee professionals.

www.misskittysjournal.com. *Miss Kitty's Journal.* A quarterly online and print magazine for Red Hatters that focuses on Victorian aspects of tea.

www.southernladymagazine.com. *Southern Lady.* A monthly magazine that always includes a section on tea.

www.catteacorner.com/teadigest.htm.—*Tea Digest.* All about tea for the consumer online.

www.TheTeaHouseTimes.com. Bi-monthly print and online magazine that covers teahouses plus up-to-date information on tea. It also runs a speakers bureau at www.TeaBureau.com .

www.teamag.com. A magazine completely devoted to tea.

Tearoom Guide & Digest. A quarterly whose editor-in-chief is James Norwood Pratt.

www.teaviews.com. Reviews of tea books and films.

www.teainfusion.com. *Tea Time Gazette.* An international newsletter.

www.teatimemagazine.com. *TeaTime Magazine.* Covers a wide range of tea subjects.

www.the-leaf.org. An interactive online tea
magazine.

Films about Tea

It's true! Tea is becoming so popular that films are
being made about tea production, tea history, giants
in the industry, and even tea operas. Following is a
selection.

Blank, Les, and Gina Leibrecht (directors). *All in
This Tea*. Flower Films, 2007.

De Lauzanne, Xavier (director). *The Lord of
Darjeeling*. Sold with the book by Rajah Banerjee
The Rajah of Darjeeling Organic Tea: Makaibari.
Delhi: Foundation Books, 2009.

Dun, Tan (composer). *Tea: A Mirror of Soul* (filmed
opera). G. Schirmer, Inc., 2002.

———. *Tea: Broken Silence* (filmed opera).
Juxtapositions Studio, 2007.

Hoyt, Scott Chamberlin. *The Meaning of Tea: A Tea
Inspired Journey*. Tea Dragon Films, 2008. Also a
book published by Talking Leaves Press, 2009.

Perelsztejn, Diane (director). *Robert Fortune: The
Tea Thief*. Belgium: Les Films de la Mémoire,
2001.

Yu, F. Lit. *The Renaissance of Tea*. Pine Wood
Studios, 2005.

Tea Rooms

Rather than list the myriads of tea rooms and teahouses around the world, I refer you to the most updated resources I know. First check out *Great Tea Rooms of America* and *Great Tea Rooms of Britain* by Bruce Richardson. (See the entries in the Bibliography for details.) Also go on line at www.teaguide.net for a tea room directory that lists thousands of venues worldwide, and which is updated frequently.

GET MORE AT **LLEWELLYN.COM**

Visit us online to browse hundreds of our books and decks, plus sign up to receive our e-newsletters and exclusive online offers.

- **Free tarot readings • Spell-a-Day • Moon phases**
- **Recipes, spells, and tips • Blogs • Encyclopedia**
- **Author interviews, articles, and upcoming events**

GET SOCIAL WITH **LLEWELLYN**

 Find us on Facebook
www.Facebook.com/LlewellynBooks

Follow us on
 twitter
www.Twitter.com/Llewellynbooks

GET BOOKS AT **LLEWELLYN**

LLEWELLYN ORDERING INFORMATION

Order online: Visit our website at www.llewellyn.com to select your books and place an order on our secure server.

Order by phone:
- Call toll free within the U.S. at 1-877-NEW-WRLD (1-877-639-9753)
- Call toll free within Canada at 1-866-NEW-WRLD (1-866-639-9753)
- We accept VISA, MasterCard, and American Express

Order by mail:
Send the full price of your order (MN residents add 6.875% sales tax) in U.S. funds, plus postage and handling to: Llewellyn Worldwide, 2143 Wooddale Drive Woodbury, MN 55125-2989

POSTAGE AND HANDLING

STANDARD: (U.S. & Canada)
(Please allow 12 business days)
$25.00 and under, add $4.00.
$25.01 and over, FREE SHIPPING.

INTERNATIONAL ORDERS (airmail only):
$16.00 for one book, plus $3.00 for each additional book.

Visit us online for more shipping options.
Prices subject to change.

FREE CATALOG!

To order, call
1-877-NEW-WRLD
ext. 8236
or visit our
website

HERB MAGIC FOR BEGINNERS

Down-to-Earth Enchantments

ELLEN DUGAN

Stir up passion with violet or nab a new job with honeysuckle. From parsley to periwinkle, people enjoy herbs for their aroma, taste, and healing abilities, but few are aware of the enchanting powers harnessed within these multipurpose plants. Breathing new life into herbal folklore and wisdom, Ellen Dugan introduces the magical side of these natural treasures.

The author of *Cottage Witchery* describes the magical traits of flowers, roots, trees, spices, and other commonly found herbs. Under her guidance, readers learn the basics of magic and spellworking so they may safely explore herbal magic on their own for health, luck, prosperity, romance, protection, and more!

978-0-7387-0837-9
216 pp., 5³⁄₁₆ x 8 $12.95

MAGICAL HOUSEKEEPING
Simple Charms & Practical Tips for Creating a Harmonious Home
TESS WHITEHURST

Every inch and component of your home is filled with an invisible life force and unique magical energy. *Magical Housekeeping* teaches readers how to sense, change, channel, and direct these energies to create harmony in their homes, joy in their hearts, and success in all areas of their lives.

In this engaging guide, energy consultant and teacher Tess Whitehurst shares her secrets for creating an energetically powerful and positive home. Written for those new to metaphysics as well as experienced magical practitioners, *Magical Housekeeping* will teach readers how to summon success, happiness, romance, abundance, and all the desires of the heart. And, by guiding them to make changes in both the seen and unseen worlds simultaneously, this dynamic and delightful book will help to activate and enhance readers' intuition and innate magical power.

978-0-7387-1985-6
240 pp., 5³⁄₁₆ x 8 $16.95

Essential Herbal Wisdom
A Complete Exploration of 50 Remarkable Herbs
Nancy Arrowsmith

Popular author and healing practitioner Nancy Arrowsmith takes readers on a fascinating, in-depth exploration of herbs in *Essential Herbal Wisdom*. Arrowsmith's friendly voice and vast knowledge of herbal applications, history, and folklore shine through in this holistic reference work. As entertaining as it is practical, this comprehensive illustrated guide covers everything from herb gathering prayers and charms to detailed herbal correspondences for fifty powerful herbs.

Each individual herb is described in detail, with tips on growing, gathering, drying, and storing, as well as on the herb's culinary virtues, cosmetic properties, medicinal merits, veterinary values, and household applications. Along with thought-provoking bits of folk history, and literary and spiritual references to herbs and nature, this directory includes step-by-step instructions on herbal dyeing, strewing, garlanding, and festooning, as well as gardening hints and seed-saving tips.

978-0-7387-1488-2
576 pp., 7 x 10 $29.95

Sun Signs & Soul Mates
An Astrological Guide to Relationships
Linda George

From deciding whether to date that flirtatious Gemini to identifying your soul's fundamental needs, this book can help you understand yourself—and your partner—through astrology. Evolutionary astrologer Linda George reveals the compatibility potential for each pairing and offers entertaining relationship clues to help you better relate to your partner. Learn about each Sun sign's strengths, challenges, behavioral quirks, and more.

978-0-7387-1558-2
240 pp., 6 x 9 $17.95

Jude's Herbal Home Remedies
Natural Health, Beauty & Home Care Secrets
Jude C. Todd, C.H., M.H.

Discover a simpler, more natural way of life. Learn to treat headaches, dandruff, insomnia, colds, muscle aches, burns, and other ailments naturally with *Jude's Herbal Home Remedies*. Written by a master herbalist, this practical guide contains more than 800 tips using many easy-to-find herbs.

Learn how cayenne pepper promotes hair growth. Discover why cranberry juice is a good treatment for asthma attacks. Begin making your own deodorants, perfumes, teas, salves, tinctures, and tonics. Also included are housecleaning tips, beauty secrets, and natural pest repellents.

978-0-87542-869-7
384 pp., 6 x 9 $18.95

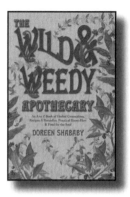

THE WILD & WEEDY APOTHECARY
An A to Z Book of Herbal Concoctions, Recipes & Remedies, Practical Know-How & Food for the Soul

DOREEN SHABABY

Step off the beaten path and into nature's wild and weedy apothecary. In this warm and friendly guide, herbalist Doreen Shababy shares her deep, abiding love for the earth and its gifts. She invites readers to be playful and adventurous as they learn how to use herbs to make a soothing salve, fragrant tea, vibrant salads, and other dishes to delight the palate as well as the eye.

This extensive collection of herbal remedies, folk and food wisdom, and eclectic recipes from around the world represents a lifetime of the author's work in the forest, field, and kitchen. Organized in an easy and fun A to Z format, Shababy's extensive knowledge of the subject and unique collection of wit and wisdom will speak to beginners and herb enthusiasts alike.

978-0-7387-1907-8
384 pp., 6 x 9 $17.95

THE STREET-SMART PSYCHIC'S GUIDE TO GETTING A GOOD READING
LISA BARRETTA

Sassy, candid, and spot-on, professional psychic Lisa Barretta offers insider advice on getting a fabulous psychic reading. Learn how to avoid charlatans and select wisely among astrologers, tarot readers, psychic phone-line services, and others. Hilarious true stories from Barretta's thirty-year career illuminate what to do—and not to do—to build a productive rapport with your reader.

978-0-7387-1850-7
312 pp., 6 x 9 $16.95

SCRYING FOR BEGINNERS
Tapping into the Supersensory Powers of Your Subconscious
DONALD TYSON

Includes special offer for a free scrying sheet.

Scrying for Beginners is for anyone who longs to sit down before the mirror or crystal and lift the rolling grey clouds that obscure their depths. Scrying is a psychological technique to deliberately acquire information by extrasensory means through the unconscious mind. For the first time, all forms of scrying are treated in one easy-to-read, practical book. They include such familiar methods as crystal gazing, pendulums, black mirrors, Ouija™ boards, dowsing rods, aura reading, psychometry, automatic writing, and automatic speaking. Also treated are ancient techniques not widely known today, such as Babylonian oil scrying, fire gazing, Egyptian lamp scrying, water scrying, wind scrying, ink scrying, shell-hearing, and oracular dreaming.

978-1-56718-746-5
320 pp., 5³⁄₁₆ x 8 $14.95

YOU ARE PSYCHIC
The Art of Clairvoyant Reading & Healing
DEBRA LYNNE KATZ

Learn to see inside yourself and others. Clairvoyance is the ability to see information—in the form of visions and images—through nonphysical means.
According to Debra Lynne Katz, anyone who can visualize a simple shape, such
as a circle, has clairvoyant ability.

In *You Are Psychic*, Katz shares her own experiences and methods for devel-
oping these clairvoyant skills. Her techniques and psychic tools are easy to follow and have been proven to work by long-time practitioners. Psychic readings,
healing methods, vision interpretation, and spiritual counseling are all covered
in this practical guide to clairvoyance.

978-0-7387-0592-7
336 pp., 6 x 9 $16.95

Spanish edition:
Tú eres psíquico
978-0-7387-0877-5 $14.95

TO ORDER, CALL 1-877-NEW-WRLD
Prices subject to change without notice
Order at Llewellyn.com 24 hours a day, 7 days a week!